BALANCE
THAT WORKS
WHEN LIFE
DOESN'T

Susie Larson

HARVEST HOUSE PUBLISHERS

EUGENE, OREGON

Cover by Terry Dugan Design, Minneapolis, Minnesota

Cover photo © Jens Lucking/Stone/Getty Images

Published in association with the literary agency of Alive Communications, Inc., 7680 Goddard Street, Ste. #200, Colorado Springs, CO 80920

Every effort has been made to insure that the information contained in this book is complete and accurate. However, neither the author nor the publisher is engaged in rendering professional advice or services to the reader, individually or in groups. The ideas and suggestions contained in this book are not intended as substitutes for consulting professionals, as appropriate. Accordingly, individual readers and groups must assume responsibility for their own actions, safety, and health and neither the author nor the publisher shall be liable or responsible for any loss, injury, or damage allegedly arising from any information or suggestion in this book.

Every effort has been made to give proper credit for all stories, poems, and quotations. If for any reason proper credit has not been given, please notify the author or publisher and proper notation will be given on future printing.

BALANCE THAT WORKS WHEN LIFE DOESN'T
Copyright © 2005 by Susie Larson
Published by Harvest House Publishers
Eugene, Oregon 97402

Library of Congress Cataloging-in-Publication Data
Larson, Susie, 1962-
    Balance that works when life doesn't / Susie Larson.
      p. cm.
    ISBN-13: 978-0-7369-1642-4
    ISBN-10: 0-7369-1642-3
    1. Christian women—Religious life.   2. Time management—Religious aspects—Christianity.
    I. Title.
BV4527.L37 2005
248.8'43—dc22   2005001899

To Kevin,
Your commitment to a life of balance
has brought healing, joy, and strength
to my life. Thank you, honey.
I'll love you forever.

To Jesus,
How can I ever thank You enough
for Your redeeming work in my
life? I love You so much.
I'll follow You forever.

Contents

Do You Ever Wonder?

I wonder why we wander from the things that nourish our souls. We wander from healthy eating, right thinking, and time with God. We wander from faithful friends, quality time, and the challenge to grow deeper. We lose the fight for what's best for us when we don't fight at all. Somehow, for some reason, our steps take us from our appointed road toward the less-than-best path for us. Do we really enjoy living a peripheral life? I don't think so. Is it easier? Perhaps it's more convenient, but I don't think it is easier. Living a life of second bests and stuck places wears on our soul and steals our joy.

On the other hand, in the moments when things line up for us, when we are doing that which we care about, passion emerges and joy returns. We find ourselves wondering, *Why did I ever let this go?* And yet we do, over and over again.

Is it that we don't care enough? I think we care a lot. But our priorities get skewed because we live in a fallen world where the currents of sin and defeat are strong, and if not resisted, will pull us under. As long as we walk this earth we will contend with the current. But this shouldn't shake us because God has made a way for us.

God is immovable; we are the ones who move. God is consistent; we have our moments. God is powerful; we are powerless without Him. All of His thoughts are pure and holy; ours can be selfish and small. We need Jesus. Just as we need oxygen to breathe, we continually need Jesus' input, His breath, and His Spirit in and through us. He is our Source. We must stay close to the Source.

How are you today? Take a moment and read through the following questions:

1. Do you wish you had more energy?
2. Do you lack focus, passion, and direction in your life?

3. Do you feel at the mercy of your schedule? Is life pulling you in too many directions?

4. Does the term "spiritual health" make you think of rigid rules and an *un-maintainable* level of holiness?

5. Would you like to be more physically fit?

6. Would you like to enjoy a greater awareness of God's love for you?

If you answered yes to any of the questions above, I ask you to join me as we explore the wonder of our physical and spiritual health. God has divinely woven them together. You must know at the outset that you are loved and accepted right where you are. But if you are interested, there is more for you!

This book is for the soul that is tired of halfhearted living. Get ready to take a fearless inventory of your habits and choices. As you read, you'll be led out of the swirling current of imbalance to a place of stability and strength in your physical and spiritual life.

You will begin to feel relieved as you find yourself "off the hook" from having to achieve a certain picture of perfection in your life. On the other hand, you will feel "back on the hook" as you are challenged in every circumstance to find the most fruitful place amid your life's season.

There are two parts to this book—physical health and spiritual health—and both will deal with essential components of health and holiness. There are study questions at the end of each chapter that can be used individually or in a group. Take your time and pray through every chapter. Allow God to speak to you, deal with you, heal you, and set you free to powerfully affect the world around you. When you are at your best, the world around you is blessed!

It is my prayer that as you read you will feel led to accept God's forgiveness and leave your past behind…and that you will trust Jesus with your future…*so that* you'll be fully alive in the present moment. May your soul be awakened to all you have in Him today—that you may be a living, breathing example of Christ's love for a lost world—so that when others encounter you, they encounter Him.

Bless the day, my sister!
Susie Larson

Part One

Physical Health

I discipline my body like an athlete,
training it to do what it should.
Otherwise, I fear that after preaching to others
I myself might be disqualified.
1 CORINTHIANS 9:27

One

How Did I Get Here?

Then Jesus said, "Come to me, all of you who are weary and carry heavy burdens, and I will give you rest. Take my yoke upon you. Let me teach you, because I am humble and gentle, and you will find rest for your souls. For my yoke fits perfectly, and the burden I give you is light."

MATTHEW 11:28-30

My GOOD INTENTIONS HAD GOTTEN THE BEST OF ME. I said yes to too many things, and now I was paying a price that was costly. I had no room in my life for red lights, wide-load trucks, or leaky dishwashers. Every minute had its place in my day as I whipped from one task to another, checking them from my list upon completion.

As my car hurried around a bend, I chomped on a dry bagel. The trees sped by in a blur. The thought, *Savor the flavor,* crossed my mind, but I waved it away as though it were a gnat that circled my head. I made it to the bank, the library, and then reached the restaurant just in time for my lunch appointment. How did I end up on this fast track again? Where did that place of peace go? I shoveled down a salad as I listened intently to my friend. *Savor.* There it was again. My friend and I shared a wonderful time, but it was over before I knew it.

A glance at my watch reminded me that I knew I still had three stops to make before heading home in time to get the kids off the bus. My friend and I embraced and promised not to let so much time pass before we would meet again. The gurgle sounds coming from my stomach made me realize that perhaps I had eaten a bit too fast. *Savor the flavor.*

I marched out to my car and got behind the wheel. Warming up the car a bit before taking off gave me an opportunity to pray. "What is it that You are trying to tell me, Lord?" The Lord spoke to my heart, *You are living in the "next" moment and missing the present one. You are so focused on your destination that you are only thinking about getting there. Did you happen to notice the beautiful sky I painted this morning? How about the trees? Did you notice how the treetops were blanketed with fresh snow? Take your salad today; you were so busy stabbing your next bite that you were totally unaware of the great morsel of food you already had in your mouth. That taste was history before it ever hit your lips. How about if you savor the flavor of the bite in your mouth? Be thankful for the abundance of food in front of you and take a moment to enjoy it. You're missing so much of the journey because your mind is on the destination.*

I wasn't sure how long I sat there, but it didn't matter. I was receiving a spiritual adjustment. Things had subtly gotten out of whack, and I was overlooking significant gifts that had been sent my way throughout the day. I decided my other errands could wait and I headed home. On the way I slowed as I rounded the bend. I looked at the lofty pines that pointed to the heavens. I even put the window down several inches just to breathe in the crisp winter air. "Thank You, Jesus, for this beautiful day."

I arrived home in time to see my kids get off the bus. Instead of rushing to get that one extra load of dishes done before they burst through the door, I went to the living room window and watched them as they hoofed through the deep snow with rosy cheeks and thick winter garb. They lobbed a few snowballs across the street to their neighbor buddies and then ducked behind a snow mound to dodge returning fire. They grow up so fast. I breathed a prayer, "Help me to make the best of these days, Lord. Help me not to race through each day, but instead see the miracles in front of me. May I remember that each day is a special gift, wrapped in a supernatural bow. Oh, and by the way, thank You for that beautiful sky...it's going to be a glorious sunset."

As I watched my kids make their way to the front door, my mind wandered back to a tougher time in our lives. We were on the cancer floor with our little boy. He was having night sweats and had a large lump on his neck. We watched as they wheeled him away for various tests. But something was different during this trial. Because of the many crises we endured in previous years, we finally believed God to be who He said He was. We truly knew that God was for us (Romans 8:31). We could take Him at His Word, and we did. Even though we were nervous and on edge, we had an inner peace and stability.

We also had many people praying for us, visiting us, and taking care of our household duties. We received great blessings from family, our church, and the hospital. I felt so cared for that even in the middle of our crisis, I had something to give away. I sat in a large rocking chair and watched all of the precious, hairless children welcome my child into the fold. I found myself asking, "What does obedience look like here, Lord? How can I love, serve, and obey You in this setting?" The Lord whispered to my heart, *Watch the other moms and dads. Look at the fatigue in their eyes and pray for them. They live this every day. Listen to them and help to carry their load.* I looked around at some of the world's greatest unsung heroes.

Life moves so fast. We have appointments, luncheons, hockey games, videos, late fees, highways, skyways, hallways, and *my way*. Here it was just the opposite: aches, pains, prayers and tears, hall-ways, dark ways, lost ways, slow days, and *not my way*. Wow. Nobody looked polished around here. They looked tired and weary. They didn't seem to notice because this was not their focus; their children were. I lost track of time as they shared their stories. I was thankful to pray for a weary grandmother and grateful to receive comfort from her as well. I had an underlying strength that held fast. This was a powerful revelation to me—I found the eye of the storm, the axis in a very stressful situation. I saw myself fully as a child of God. I was under His care, but I was also under His charge. And since I had strength to give, He provided the opportunity to serve.

Somehow I had found my place of balance in that crisis (thank-fully, our son *didn't* end up having cancer). And yet here in *this* place and time, watching my healthy boys get off the bus, I realized that by overcommitting myself, I gave too much away, and with it, my sense of wonder. God called me back once again to find my peace with Him in the season I was in.

Balance Is More Than Skin Deep

Now, granted, there are times of crisis when we need to receive far more than we are capable of giving out. There are also times of strength and grace when we can give much more than we are receiving at the time. But we cannot go for too long, giving at the expense of the receiving, without losing our health and perspective. And we must never let go of the fact that we are living, breathing creatures made for a heavenly kingdom. God always provides nourishment for our souls; He also sets up many divine appointments where we can offer a blessing; and He paints many beautiful skies that call us to lay down and look up.

True balance isn't defined by the appearance of having it all together. Some of the most together-looking women are the most out of balance—at least from a heavenly point of view. In the worldly sense, self-realization and self-ambition have become true-blue idols. The pursuit of elevating one's self, gifts, and abilities has become a respectable and acceptable road in the secular arena. But as women of faith who love our Savior, we are called to a much different path. He is the point, He is the One who gets the credit, and He is the One we serve.

The irony is that as we embrace the God-given components of a healthy life, we *will* look more put together. We will *have* more together. But this won't be our highest aim because we know better than anyone how quickly life can change. Our goal and our aim is to pursue the mind-set that we are *alive* in Christ. He wants to breathe life into us so that we can serve Him by living a healthy and holy life. We are promised in Scripture that we will encounter trials and troubles. Yet we are also promised access to the very power that raised Christ from the dead (Ephesians 1:19-20).

Since Christ has paid for and provided for every scenario, we have all we need to embrace life with a sense of purpose, power, and balance. This kind of balance goes with us and adjusts to the places God takes us and to the things He allows to happen in our lives.

Balance Is Worth Pursuing

Where are you right now? It doesn't matter if your road is rough or smooth. There is balance to be found and greater health to be realized. Even in the valley, there is higher ground—the place of greatest fruitfulness—and it is *that* place we seek in every situation. As we move along in our journey toward balance, you will receive practical tips that will help you both physically and spiritually. You will be challenged to go just a bit further than you may feel like going. If you apply the principles in this book, you will get healthier, but more importantly, you will gain a heavenly perspective that will allow you to find your place with Jesus no matter where life finds you.

Father God,

You have done so much for me, and I thank You with all my heart. I don't know why I sometimes choose the less-than-best path when I know there is a better way. Motivate me to start anew today. Help me to find my way to the peace You provide. I want to take what You have given and give You a great return on Your investment. Create in me an excitement to live a healthier life. I love You. Amen.

Steps Toward Health

* If my life is currently caught in the swirling current, I will come before God today and find my place of peace with Him. I will ask Him to show me what needs to go from my schedule.

* If my life is currently a peaceful, balanced place, I will thank God today for blessing me in this way. I will ask the Lord to show me practical ways to guard the balance I am enjoying right now while looking for opportunities to stretch, grow, and to be a blessing to the world around me.

- I will be mindful that there is a fine line between a healthy protection of my balance and a selfish protection of my personal comforts. I will ask the Lord to heighten my conviction so that I will instantly notice when I begin to approach the "selfish line."

- I will ask the Lord to prepare me to take this journey toward health and holiness. I will stand in faith, knowing He will come through for me.

TRY THIS

- If you feel hopelessly overcommitted while looking at this month's calendar, sit down and pray. Ask the Lord to show you what can be rescheduled or taken off your schedule. Make the phone calls and the necessary adjustments.

- Look at your calendar and "X" off a day or two each week where you plan not to have plans, especially those days that fall right before or right after an event or a commitment that may deplete you.

- Write down a list of five high-priority items you want to accomplish this month (for example, a date with my child, catch up on paperwork, visit a grandparent). Post that short list next to your monthly calendar. When you receive calls and requests for commitments, measure those requests against the things you felt convicted to accomplish at the beginning of your month. Guard your time and accomplish the things you know you should.

Balance Application

If life is too busy, make the adjustments to find your place of peace again. If you are in a crisis, whether it feels natural or not, seek after God and find your place with Him so you are not swept away with your fears. Some crises are so intense that the Lord Himself carries us through without any pressing in on our part. If you are on a smooth path, guard it and look for ways to be a blessing to others.

Study Time

1. Read Ruth 2:8-22 in your Bible.

2. Do you see a parallel with Boaz's care for Ruth and your heavenly Father's care for you? Explain.

3. In what tangible ways did Boaz equip and care for Ruth?

4. Why was it important for Ruth to stay within the boundaries set for her?

5. Why is it important for you to do the same?

6. Ruth was a woman of honor, hard work, humility, and gratitude. In what ways do you see God establishing these virtues in you?

7. Pause and pray. Ask the Lord to draw you closer to Him.

Two
What Balance Isn't

*There has never been the slightest doubt in
my mind that the God who started this great
work in you would keep at it and bring it to
a flourishing finish on the very day Christ
Jesus appears.*

Philippians 1:6 MSG

I TRIED TO REST, BUT I COULDN'T. THE PAIN kept me from falling
into a deep sleep. I looked once more at the needle pokes up and
down my arms and sighed. My veins were collapsing, requiring new
sites for the IV. I stared at the plastic cylinder imbedded in my arm.
Attached to it was a long tube that reached up to a bag of medicine,
which hung on the miniblinds behind the couch. The medicine was
a mixed bag of blessings and curses. On the one hand, the fluid in
that bag was my only hope for recovery. On the other hand, it was
costing us a fortune and forcing us deeper into debt. The medicine
made me sick, weak, and tired, but it was also supposed to make me
better.

Whenever I think back to that time in my life—battling Lyme disease—I find myself full of thanks. My life never looked as imbalanced as it did back then. Rather than teaching aerobics classes, my

extra exertion was taking a shower...once a week. More than that would have taken energy I didn't possess. Our house was falling apart, our debt was growing, and many different people were caring for my three little boys because I was too sick to do so.

I find myself thankful because it was in that terrible valley that I learned surrender, brokenness, and trust. I had to face the promise I had made long ago when I gave my life to Jesus. Was I serious about my commitment to Him when it seemed He was answering none of my prayers? After many tears, I decided I was serious about my heart's cry for more of Him and less of me. The hardest part for me was my inability to produce *anything*. In fact, I was costing money, time, resources, and energy. There was nothing I could do about it, and for a "doer," this was a nightmare come true.

And yet it was only in my depletion where I could have found God to be my *everything*. As I faced the black hole of insecurity that hid beneath all my efforts, I found that God's love fills every empty place (when we're not filling them with something else). He *is* the Source of identity, of hope, and of life itself. Had I not plummeted to the depths of despair and sickness, I would not have been able to grasp the scope of His love and care for His people.

We live in a society that measures value by what one produces and how many titles one claims. But we cannot and must not allow such a shallow measure to define something God has created. Though from the outside I looked as though I was wasting away... costing much, contributing little...that valley provided my life's highest education.

Because God went to great lengths to create in you something that has never been done before or ever will be again, you must let *Him* decide your worth. Because He is the one who knows best how you are wired, may He be the one who becomes your point of reference (this is something we'll look at in depth later in the book).

"Our lives are a fragrance presented by Christ to God. But this fragrance is perceived differently by those being saved and by those perishing" (2 Corinthians 2:15). We measure our lives by a different standard because our highest goal is not to be accepted by the world, but to bring pleasure to God.

Before we can maintain a godly balance in our lives, we must first define what balance isn't.

Balance Is Not...A Put-Together Appearance

Women who appear extremely put together can sometimes be the most imbalanced of persons. When emphasis is placed on perfecting outward presentation, it can be at the expense of true personal growth. Women who work too hard to appear perfectly together will tell me they do so because there is another area in their lives that feels completely out of control.

Some women, however, just have a knack for keeping it all together...God bless 'em. I sometimes think one reason those women were put on this earth is to keep the rest of us humbly dependent on Jesus. There is a wonderful consolation here, though. As you pursue a life of godly balance and health, you will *look* more together and you will *have* more together. But this should not be our goal. Being fully alive in Christ is our goal. As we gain ground both physically and spiritually, we will hold what we love with an open hand, fully trusting Jesus' work in our lives. The pursuit of God with a posture of trust keeps us positioned and prepared for all that comes our way.

Balance Is Not...A Perfectly Managed Schedule

There is no getting around the need for calendars, PDAs, and day planners. Due to our multifaceted life, we need to keep our planners updated as well as keep them from being inundated. Again, there are those who are punctual; perfect managers of their appointments, arrivals, and departures. There is great virtue in being organized and prompt. I once heard someone say, "Being late is a form of selfishness; I'm basically saying that I care more about my schedule than I do yours." Ouch. Very true.

To be frantic, harried, and forgetful of where we are supposed to be and when we're supposed to be there certainly undermines our witness. However, balance is not simply a perfectly managed schedule. In fact, some of the best schedule managers I have ever seen forget about little things like, say...people! When it is all said and done, people and God are the only things that will last, and if we spend our days serving and mastering our schedules we will miss the needs of those around us. When this happens, we lose, and those we were appointed to touch lose as well.

While managing our schedule is a component to balance, true balance also has a flexibility and adaptability to it. True balance makes the plan but allows the Lord to determine the steps (Proverbs 16:9). Moreover, as you begin to maintain balance, your schedule will feel more doable and you will have more margin in your life.

Balance Is Not...A Life Free of Conflict and Difficulty

There is a big difference between the peacekeeper and the peacemaker. The peacekeeper works tirelessly to avoid conflict in order to preserve the *appearance* that "all is well, no conflict here." The peacemaker is determined to have true inner peace and will therefore live from the truth and deal openly and honestly with conflict. James 3:17-18 says, "But the wisdom that comes from heaven is first of all pure. It is also peace loving, gentle at all times, and willing to yield to others. It is full of mercy and good deeds. It shows no partiality and is always sincere. And those who are peacemakers will plant seeds of peace and reap a harvest of goodness."

A life of balance pursues a heart of peace. This world is full of fallen, sinful people, and there will be conflict. The question is, will you come through it more pure, holy, and forgiving? Or will you harbor bitterness and poison your soul? A truly balanced woman will face conflict with dignity, security, humility, and love.

In order to keep balance and perspective in all seasons, we must dispel the picture from our mind that calls us to be "on" in every situation. God is much more merciful than that. And yet His provision is so abundant that He, being "on" all of the time, will powerfully work through us even in our lowest of times. Balance is not summed up by the picture of what is happening on the outside. It is dictated by the truth that is transforming us on the inside.

Precious Lord,

You are all that I need. You are my strength and my portion. Help me, Lord, not to look to the latest fad or fashion to determine my worth. May I never judge my value by what I produce. Help me instead see things from Your perspective. As I embrace Your values and make them my own, I will begin to change from the inside out. Give me a clearer picture of what balance looks like for me in this season that I'm in. Protect me from the sin of comparison and help me fix my eyes on You. I need You every hour. Amen.

Steps Toward Health

* If I am currently in a valley, I will resist the temptation to compare myself with those who are not. I will say, "Okay, I can't do _____, but I can do _____."

* If I am currently in a place of peace and plenty, I will resist the

temptation to think that life is good because I am good. Life is good because God is good, and I will use my strength to help someone who needs a hand.

* I will change my thinking (if necessary) in regards to what a "successful day" looks like. I will try to be open and flexible toward the changing needs of each new day.

TRY THIS

* Write down the five things you value most in this world. Do your time investments reflect your values?

* Take some extra time this week and spend it in prayer. Ask the Lord to give you a sense of what He is working on in you. Write it down, tuck it in your Bible, and continually pray about it until you see maturity in that area.

* Take a personal inventory of your motivations. Is there anything you are consistently doing, pursuing, or putting time to so that others will think _____? Ask the Lord to help you step away from this thing and allow that empty place to be filled by Him.

* Meditate this week on the fact that God loves you just for who you are and not for what you've accomplished. Allow yourself to be filled with joy at the thought of it. Once you've taken hold of this truth, don't let it get away from you.

Balance Application

All of us to some degree are products of our environment, and yet as one of my favorite authors, Francis Frangipane, has said, "We must determine to allow nothing and no one to shape us, not even our personal experiences—unless they are consistent with the promises of God." To live within the promises of God, we must guard our hearts from the poison of bitterness. To maintain true balance, we must honestly assess our circumstance and then look for and find the place of greatest fruitfulness; this is how we gain ground even in the deepest valleys.

Study Time

1. Think about Ruth again for a moment. She was a widow in a foreign land who worked long hours under the sun to help provide for her mother-in-law and herself. Ruth did not have an easy life, but she truly was a woman of honor. Read Ruth 4:13-17.

2. Describe in your own words Ruth's struggles and the outcome.

3. How often do you notice God making something magnificent out of something menial? (Write down or discuss other times you've seen this happen in the Bible and in modern-day life.)

4. Where are you at in your own process (for example, waiting, working, reaping)?

5. How is your attitude in relation to where you are right

now? (If you are struggling, be honest about it. Ask for prayer and allow God to speak to your heart.)

6. To give a "sacrifice of praise" is to thank and worship God even when it is difficult to do. The sacrifice of praise puts feelings aside and hangs on to faith instead. Giving God the thanks He deserves will sometimes cost us something. Pause and thank Him by faith for His promise to meet *all* of your needs. He is still faithful and He will make something beautiful of your life if you let Him.

Three
What Balance Is

All of us must quickly carry out the tasks assigned to us by the one who sent me, because there is little time left before the night falls and all work comes to an end.

JOHN 9:4

W HEN I THINK BACK TO THE TIMES I was most out of balance both physically and spiritually, I shudder. Those were the times in my life when I was most depleted and distracted. Twenty-plus years ago when I was carrying 35 extra pounds, my weight (and my stomach hanging over my jeans) was the first thing I thought about in the morning and the last thing I fretted about at night. Was I a fruitful Christian back then? I believe so, but not nearly as fruitful as I could have been because I was imprisoned and distracted by my own physical imbalance.

My mind also recalls a time when I was spiritually out of whack. I did too many things, and I am quite sure that I did few of them well. I can laugh now when I think back to whipping out the door with my jacket hanging by one sleeve and my arms wrapped around my purse, my Bible, and my planner. My keys are in my mouth, and

I am yelling through pursed lips, "Dinner is in the oven!" I imagine my new neighbor walking by in fascination and wondering, *Wow, who's that gal? I want what she has!"*

Through painful circumstances beyond my control as well as messes I've made for myself, I have finally found a form of balance that works even when life doesn't. Through pressing into the Lord during times of testing, I learned a profound concept. I pray I can communicate it in a way that you can quickly take hold of and apply.

Encarta Dictionary defines balance this way: A state in which various elements form a satisfying and harmonious whole and *nothing is out of proportion or unduly emphasized at the expense of the rest* (emphasis added).

Now that we have put away the notion that the balanced woman is one who keeps it together at all times, we can examine the true components of balance.

The True Components of Balance

Everyone's life involves these three things to some degree (I will interchange these terms throughout the book):

1. Input (Nourishment)
2. Output (Response)
3. Rest (Replenishment)

When either input or output is unduly emphasized at the expense of the rest, you have imbalance. Let's look at these three components as the three levers in life. As long as you live, you will be receiving nourishment, responding to what's been deposited in you, and resting from your labors (both physically and spiritually). What will change through the varying seasons of life is the *degree* that you do these things.

When I was sick in bed, I couldn't even consider training to run a race. I could, however, do range of motion with my joints so I wouldn't get arthritis. Though my output when compared to a healthy person seemed like a dismal failure, for me it was maximizing my potential. Applying myself to that small task took care of my joints—and now I am able to run 5K races. As I mentioned earlier, part of holding your ground (and gaining it) is honestly assessing your circumstance and then finding the greatest place of fruitfulness in the midst of it all. In every situation, there is the best way to nourish yourself, the best way to respond to what's been deposited in you, and the best way to be replenished again.

We wander away from balance when we neglect, forget, or think we don't need all three of these components in our lives. We can't eat a lot and never exercise, we can't exert ourselves constantly without food, and we can't neglect rest.

As we come to understand the components of balance, we will also come to grasp the *fluidity* of balance. In other words, these components will adjust to our seasons and circumstances of life.

Throughout much of this book, we will look at our physical and spiritual nourishment (input), our physical and spiritual exercise (output), and our physical and spiritual replenishment (rest). You will be given tangible tips that will help you hold your ground on the bad days and gain new ground on the good days. At first glance, one would think that a book on balance should address how we juggle all of our roles in life. To me, this is like managing the symptoms. If we take a deeper look at what comes into our lives, what goes out from us, and how we get replenished again—if we manage our lives at *this* level—we will get to the core of where we put our time and why.

As we develop the mind-set that God has great nourishment for us physically and spiritually, we will become more alive in Christ.

We will go through our days with a sense of expectation, knowing that He has things He wants to deposit in us. We will pause and really taste the food He has provided for us (physical input), and we will marvel at the creative ways He speaks to us throughout the day (spiritual input). We will also come to understand our responsibility as His children to be open and ready to be used by Him wherever and whenever He says. We will exercise our physical body and bring it into a healthy balance, and we will stretch ourselves spiritually to affect the world around us (physical and spiritual output). Finally, we will understand the command for rest—a blessed gift from a Father who knows what we need (physical and spiritual replenishment).

When we live with the constant sense of the ebb and flow of nourishment, response, and replenishment we will find balance wherever life finds us.

A Balanced Woman Is...

* Someone who, even though she is cleaning the house to prepare for company, takes her little ones outside and runs around with them for a while.

* Someone who would rather bless than impress (wise words from my pastor's wife).

* Someone who dares to say no to something she's not called to, even though she might disappoint others.

* Someone who senses a call on her life and dares to say yes, even though she feels unqualified.

* Someone who guards and protects her time spent with the Lord.

* Someone who gives herself the gift of exercising several times per week.

- Someone who is willing to interrupt her workout if a friend needs prayer or her child needs a hug.

- Someone who, several times a day, pauses to acknowledge God's presence.

- Someone who, even in crisis or a valley, will look for God's purpose and count on His provision.

- Someone who refuses a busied, harried lifestyle.

- Someone who gives herself (and her children) plenty of time to get out the door.

- Someone who is willing to push herself beyond what's comfortable for the purpose of growth.

- Someone who is teachable.

- Someone who is flexible.

- Someone who has self-control.

- Someone who hates gossip.

- Someone who loves peace.

- Someone who looks at difficult people with God in mind.

- Someone who holds tight to faith, hope, and love.

Father God,

You have provided everything I need to live a life of fullness. Overwhelming victory is mine because of Your power. May I live from that place of power rather than defeat. Help me lay hold of all You have made available to me. I long to be balanced, unhurried, fruitful, and at peace. Bring me to that place of promise. In Your precious name I pray. Amen.

Steps Toward Health

* In relation to the three levers in life, input, output, and rest, I will take an honest look at whether a lever has been unduly emphasized in my life.

* I will ask God to show me the most tangible way to maintain balance in this area.

* I will share this pursuit with a godly friend and ask for feedback.

* I will remember that it took a series of choices to lead me out of balance, and it will take a series of good choices to lead me back again.

* I will remind myself every single day that I am on the path to greater physical and spiritual health.

TRY THIS

* Plan within the next couple days to get out and take a brisk 45 minute walk. Start to make this a habit.

* Try going to bed a little earlier tonight. If you have little ones, allow yourself to rest during their nap.

* This week, eat less and pray more. See what happens.

* Try saying no when you know you should.

* At the end of each week, do a "balance inventory" and make note of what you did well and where you still need to grow.

Balance Application

With the demands of life pressing in on all sides, it is far too easy to lose touch with issues such as nourishment, response, and replenishment. And yet, this is at the root of all we do and why. When we look closely at what we put in our bodies (and our souls), how (or if) we exercise, and to what extent we replenish ourselves, we will see a very clear picture of why we feel the way we do. Once we learn and apply the very basic components of a healthy, balanced life, we give ourselves the gifts of strength, perspective, energy, and room to grow.

Study Time

1. In 1 Samuel 1 we read about Hannah, a woman deeply loved by her husband, Elkanah, but who was barren in her womb. Hannah was teased and tormented by Peninnah, Elkanah's other wife, who was able to have children. This broke Hannah's heart, and she cried out to God for mercy. Read 1 Samuel 1:19-27.

2. When Hannah's prayers were answered, what did she do?

3. Now read 1 Samuel 2:1-10.

4. As you read Hannah's prayer of praise, meditate on the sovereignty of God. What are at least four truths you can glean from this passage and apply to your own life?

5. When you think of God being fully in control, are you able to trust Him with the things that weigh you down and stress you out? If not, why not?

6. Pray for an increased sense of His presence in your life.

Four

You're Not in Over Your Head

Stand up and praise the LORD your God,
who is from everlasting to everlasting.

NEHEMIAH 9:5 NIV

I PULLED MY HOOD OVER MY HEAD AS THE winds blew and the gray clouds began to shift. I watched the ocean waves gather momentum just before crashing against the pier. This was not ideal weather for a day at the ocean, but my boys begged to try surfing just once before our vacation was over.

The strength and the force of the waves surprised me as I nervously watched my young sons fumble for balance on their surfboards. Thankfully, they stayed close to shore and were well within my reach should I need to get to them.

Another gust of wind swept my bookmark into the air. I chased it down and put it back in its place. Just as I glanced up again, I noticed a panicked look on both Jake's and Luke's faces. My heart rate sped up as I watched the undercurrent quickly sweep them farther from the shore. They paddled and paddled with their hands, but to no avail. The strength of the water pulled them far out of reach.

Just as I was getting ready to run to them, the lifeguard stood up and put a megaphone to his mouth. He yelled, "You two boys on the boards, don't panic! Just stand up! Just stand up! The water is only four feet deep even way out there. You can do it. Stand up!"

Jake and Luke looked up at the lifeguard and decided to listen to him. Even though they were far from shore and being tossed to and fro by strong waves, they hopped off their boards into the water and found solid ground beneath their feet. They pressed through the current and within moments were safely ashore. It was as simple as that.

Choosing to Stand Up

Even though Jake and Luke *meant* to stay close to the beach, they were carried 30 yards from shore. Things looked a little scary, and the situation *seemed* over their heads, but they found their way back simply by standing up. That's what we are going to do today.

Imagine if I would have said to myself, *Oh well, my boys are too far out of reach now. I can't get to them. I will really miss them.* Of course, that is preposterous, and human life is far more valuable than any health goals we may have...and yet, how often do we allow ourselves to give up and let go of things God wants us to have?

The enemy of our souls whispers words of defeat in our ears, and we are often quick to believe him. We've all heard familiar words like, "You'll never catch up now" or "Now you've blown it" or "Why can't you get it together?" or "You have no self-control!" Every one of these statements is in direct conflict with the Word of God. Even if we have messed up or struggle with self-control, God's promises are *for us,* today, right here, right now. It took me a long time to learn to refuse to listen to such defeating thoughts, but as I filled my mind with the promises of God, my whole perspective changed.

It all starts with our perspective of where we are now and where we *could* be. Dear sister, wherever you are, God has more for you. Maybe you intended to keep your weight within a healthy range, but the currents of life have swept you to a place that feels out of control. Or maybe your weight is fine, but you know that God is calling you to a healthier diet so you will feel better and live stronger. Perhaps you are in a spiritual rut and longing for fresh nourishment from God that will strengthen you spiritually. Well, you are in the right place!

Today we are going to declare that we are not as out of control as we may feel. The road back to health isn't an unattainable one; it just requires that we face the current that swirls about us, jump in right where we are, and determine to stand on what we know to be true. We can do this.

Nourishing My Physical Body

It's always good for us to remember that food is a gift from God. Food is meant for the nourishment of our bodies, the repairing of cells for the promotion of health, energy storage, and for *occasional* enjoyment. Some of our fondest memories have been centered on breaking bread and sharing a meal with our loved ones. Unfortunately, we sometimes put too much emphasis on satisfying our taste buds and have thus lost the essence of the purpose of food. God is our Source—food is a gift. When we look to food as our source, we fall out of balance.

Let's look at what food is *not* for.

Food is not for drowning our sorrows. "Surely he took up our infirmities and carried our sorrows" (Isaiah 53:4 NIV). Jesus carries our sorrows. He will go to the source of our ache and bring healing and truth there if we ask Him to. He will bring freedom and clarity where there is pain and confusion. Our kids will at times break our hearts, friends sometimes betray, and loved ones eventually pass on. But food in this case will not serve as nourishment. In fact, it will *stand* in the way of the nourishment that comes from God. When you are overcome with sadness or sorrow, try praying and fasting instead. Or sit in God's presence with a notebook and write down what He speaks to your heart.

Food is not an outlet for our anger. "Refrain from anger and turn from wrath; do not fret—it leads only to evil" (Psalm 37:8 NIV). Eating when you are angry only feeds your inability to practice self-restraint in difficult situations. I remember one day years ago when my boys were little and they were at each other all day long. The dog had a bladder infection, which caused obvious problems, and the neighbor boy purposely put a handful of gravel in our pool because he heard it would stop up the filter. On top of that, the city was flushing the fire hydrants, which caused my load of white clothes to be covered in rust spots. I was beside myself with anger and frustration. Many times in the past, a day like this would prompt me to pull out a carton of ice cream and a spoon. But I was determined to overcome my unhealthy habits and even more determined to find out what God's power could do in my real-life tough situations. I learned that eating when you are angry doesn't help the situation. Next time you're mad and find yourself reaching for food, get away from the kitchen, go for a brisk walk, and pray.

Food is not a cure for boredom. "Restore to me the joy of your salvation and grant me a willing spirit, to sustain me" (Psalm 51:12 NIV). The next time you're tempted to eat because you are bored, try calling someone who needs a word of encouragement, bring the neighbor a bouquet of flowers, or do whatever else God puts on your heart.

Food is not only meant to fuel us. It is for enjoyment too. "Nehemiah said, 'Go and enjoy choice food and sweet drinks, and send some to those who have nothing prepared. This day is sacred to our Lord. Do not grieve, for the joy of the LORD is your strength'" (Nehemiah 8:10 NIV). There are times when we are called to celebrate and enjoy food. These events provide us with great release, encouragement, and a reminder of the Lord's faithfulness. When we take a vacation, we plan for it, save for it, and look forward to it with great anticipation. Vacations are sweet because they are a departure from our normally busy lives. In the same way, party foods and desserts are something to "budget" and plan. As our healthy, balanced diet becomes a way of life, we will be able to fully enjoy and embrace times of celebration.

Father in heaven,

I'm thankful that nothing is too hard for You. Even if things seem out of control, they never are. I want to pursue a balanced life. Give me the courage to step through the waves of impulse and put my feet on solid ground. Increase my knowledge and understanding of what it means to live a healthy, holy life. I don't want to make my body an idol where it becomes my obsession and focus. I want to make such good choices that I will no longer be distracted by my health. I want my health to serve me so I can better serve You. Amen.

Steps Toward Health

- I will take an honest look at when and why I eat. If I consistently go toward food when I could be going toward God, I will pause and pray. I will ask for forgiveness, and then I'll ask for the grace to choose wisely from now on.

- If the way I eat happens to be an area in which I am disciplined,

I will be thankful and pray for a friend who struggles with food.

* I will put my foot down on the promises of God, do His will, and know that I will be safe. Pick a promise from the Bible and stand on it. Need a verse? Try this one: "For I can do everything with the help of Christ who gives me the strength I need" (Philippians 4:13).

TRY THIS

* When you notice the stress level picking up in your day, get away from the kitchen or the candy aisle and find a place to pray. You will truly be refreshed.

* Take a moment each morning to commit your day to the Lord. Ask Him for added grace to change your eating habits. Ask for a heightened sensitivity to His Spirit so that you will notice when you're about to grab food without thinking about it.

* Practice self-restraint in other areas of your life (for example, phone, gossip, TV, reading junk, shopping, computer games, Internet surfing, e-mail). Self-restraint takes practice, but I know you can do it.

Balance Application

As we continue to grow in the Lord, we will find ourselves turning to Him for our soul's deepest needs. In the book of Jeremiah it says that the heavens shrink back in horror when they see us drinking from "muddy puddles" when Jesus is the wellspring of life (my own paraphrase). I try to imagine the cloud of witnesses shrinking back in shock every time I looked to something other than God to medicate my pain. The heavens can't imagine why we wouldn't draw from the Source that is free and perfect. If our lives have been out of balance with too much dietary input, may we bend our knee before the Lord and recommit ourselves to finding our fullness in Him.

Study Time

1. More important than the food we do or do not eat is a heart set on obeying God. Read Daniel 1:8-20.

2. Why would it have seemed natural for Daniel to indulge in food that was not God's best for him?

3. Again, once in a while, party foods are great—but how often do you allow yourself indulgences that are less than God's best for you simply because of your surroundings?

4. Something happens spiritually when we set our hearts on doing God's will—when we say no to ourselves so we can say yes to God. Look again at the passage in Daniel. Describe some of Daniel's God-given gifts.

5. How did Daniel's gifts affect the spiritual climate around him?

6. Much of what comforts the flesh weakens the soul. Is there an excess indulgence in your life that can be replaced with a more earnest pursuit of God's purpose and power? Imagine how this would affect things around you.

7. Pray for more of Him and less of you.

Five

Be Nourished

Feast there in the Presence of GOD, your God. Celebrate everything that you and your families have accomplished under the blessing of GOD, your God.

<small>DEUTERONOMY 12:7 MSG</small>

W<small>HEN WAS THE LAST TIME YOU TRULY</small> enjoyed a meal? I am not talking about the last time you ate food that simply tasted good. When was the last time you sat down before a meal (determining to do no other tasks at the same time) and took in all of the aspects of that meal: the taste, the time, the provision? There is something powerful about pausing before a meal long enough to feel overwhelmed by the goodness of God. Isn't it something that you not only get to eat a warm meal, but you also have a choice in what foods to eat? While there are millions who are starving, you have been provided for. Do you make it a habit to embrace a heart of gratitude because of that fact? Think of how it feels after you have had the flu. That first bite of real food tastes like a treasure. Back when I was very sick and every area of my life seemed to be falling apart, I wrote this in my journal, *Thank You, Lord, for taking away. For when we have again, we know to be thankful.*

Scientific studies have proven that a thankful heart is good for our health. This is wonderful, but even more importantly, a thankful heart keeps us acknowledging God's presence and provision in everything we do. Food tastes so much better when we pause for a moment, pray for those who have less than us, thank the Lord for His provision, and then acknowledge that blessing by *tasting* each bite that nourishes us.

When we invite Jesus into our lives and ask Him to bring health and wholeness, He will do far beyond all we could ask or think (Ephesians 3:20 NKJV). We are not destined for struggle or to just get by. No, "overwhelming victory" belongs to us because we belong to Him (Romans 8:37).

Do not look down at your inability...look up at Him. We need to raise our expectation of what God will do for us even in this area of nourishing ourselves. God's promises are rich and true for every area of our lives. C.S. Lewis wrote,

> Indeed, if we consider the unblushing promises of reward and the staggering nature of the rewards promised in the Gospels, it would seem that Our Lord finds our desires, not too strong, but too weak. We are half-hearted creatures, fooling about with drink and sex and ambition when infinite joy is offered us, like an ignorant child who wants to go on making mud pies in a slum because he cannot imagine what is meant by the offer of a holiday at the sea. We are far too easily pleased.[1]

The purpose of eating right is to be nourished and strengthened to live a healthy, fruitful life. It's okay to treat ourselves occasionally. It's okay to have popcorn for dinner once in a while, but as a rule, food must not master us. It must not defeat or distract us. God has a high calling on our lives, and we cannot afford to be distracted and addicted to the things of this world. What goes in us will eventually catch up with us—so we need to be careful about what we feed ourselves. Let's look at some tangible tips for healthy eating.

Food Laws to Live By

Stay away from fad diets. Begin to think more about a lifestyle change. We live in such a quick fix society that we have come to refuse anything less than a quick solution. But quick solutions quickly fade. Anything worth having takes time to acquire. Discipline with food is definitely worth having. The goal is to have your input balance your output. Change your thinking to *I am going to take control of what I put in my mouth. I will not be at the mercy of the moment. God has made a way for me.*

Give up soda (or at least cut back). Soda is a hot button, and you will have to decide for yourself about this one. I used to be an avid consumer of diet soda, but when I was so sick I wanted to die, I learned a few things about what it means to "treat myself." Every time I treated myself to soda I was draining my bone strength, making it difficult for my body to absorb certain nutrients, depriving myself of water, and losing my taste for water and juice. Plus, it is very hard to lose weight while still getting proper nourishment if soda is a part of your diet. You decide. Even less is better.

Drink plenty of water. Water does wonders for us. From aiding in metabolism to lubricating our joints, from transporting wastes to regulating our body temperature, water works *for* us in the way that soda works against us. Often women will retain water when they don't drink enough water. I encouraged my husband to start with this one discipline in his pursuit toward health, and in five weeks he had lost ten pounds.

Budget treats. If I eat a candy bar in a dark closet, is it still fattening? I used to do mental gymnastics in an effort to justify my choices. We touched on budgeting treats earlier, but just a reminder—when you plan for treats, you can eat them out in the open without shame or guilt…and they taste so much better that way.

Keep it colorful. Don't overload on any one food item. Carrots are a great food, but if you eat too many of them, you will turn orange. Make sure you eat a nice balance of fruits, vegetables, grains, and proteins. There are varying opinions as to how one should combine these foods. Listen to your body (and your intestines). You will know if something agrees with you or not. Keep your portions small and never eat to the point of feeling stuffed.

Minimize artificial sweetener intake. This obviously doesn't apply to diabetics or others with health issues. It is also important to note that this is just my opinion. You decide and talk it over with your doctor. If you are a basically healthy person, I would encourage you to keep your artificial sweetener intake to a minimum. We still do not know all of the effects these sweeteners will have on our long-term health. Also, ingesting too many foods with artificial sweetener creates the illusion that you can eat more than you should. It is better to get used to smaller portions and healthier food choices.

Remember the metabolic rule. If you go longer than about three hours without eating, your metabolism will start to drop. Your body thinks it is going into famine and therefore provides for itself by slowing down the rate you burn calories. This will keep you alive if you are stranded in the wilderness, but if you are not truly in a famine, you will gain weight because you won't be as quick to burn up calories. It is best to have some kind of small protein snack between meals (nuts, nutritional bar, yogurt, protein shake, apples and peanut butter, etc.). This will keep your metabolism where you want it. Also, you won't be as hungry when you get to your next mealtime, which will help to keep you from eating more than you need.

Choose vitamins and supplements wisely. It's important to educate yourself on vitamins and herbs because not all of them are right for you. Just as each of us is different from the other, our strengths and deficiencies will also vary. Some herbs will help one person and make another sick. Some herbs are harmful if mixed with other herbs, and certain vitamins can be toxic when taken in large doses. Supplementing your diet is great because you are probably not getting all of the nourishment you need from food—but it is equally important to do your homework and find the supplements that are right for you.

Don't eat at night. Again, make this a rule rather than the exception. Determine not to eat after 8:00 PM and stick to it. Once you get used to it, I guarantee you will sleep better, feel better in the morning, and more easily manage your weight. If you want, give yourself a break on the weekends.

Practice partial fasts. This seems to be in conflict with the metabolic rule, but let me explain. More important than our metabolism is a heart that is not bound by habit, addiction, or selfishness. If there are areas in our lives that we dance around, make provision for, and demand that we have, it's good to take a look at those areas. When we lay those things at the altar for the purpose of having more of Christ's influence in our lives, something powerful happens. I even put this into practice with my kids when they were young. When I would notice a certain video game, toy, or TV show becoming so important to them that they were ugly if they didn't get it, I showed them that they indeed *could* live without their treasured item. After a few days I could see relief on the faces of my boys, as though they had conquered something themselves. Now as teenagers, they are quick to notice whenever something becomes more important to them than their relationship with Christ. You can fast from food,[2] from the phone, from TV, from sweets, or simply from talking too much. Every time you lift something up to the Lord and say, "Lord, here. Please take this thing so I can have more of You," you will find yourself more blessed and free than you were before (I always ask God to take care of my metabolism during my partial fasts—and He always does). If you are pregnant, nursing, diabetic, or have certain medical problems, fast from things rather than food.

Use your strength. When you feel strong, use that strength to make the best choices in your diet. When you feel weak, don't absolve yourself from making good choices. Just pray, do your best, and hang on until the storm has passed. Years ago when I was on a never-ending diet cycle, I would blow it on a Wednesday and say "Oh, well. I'll start again on Monday," giving myself four more days to eat too much. When you really think about it, we blow it for a *moment.* We don't need to count the whole day a loss. In fact, if we acknowledge it as a moment, we can adjust our "output" by getting a little more exercise and really not losing any ground. Still, try to resist the temptation of continually relying on exercise to make up for overindulging. The tendency to overeat must be conquered in your life, and it can be.

Life Laws to Be Strengthened By

Use your strength. Apply this law in life as well. On the days you feel good, bake an extra meal, clean out a closet, or do an involved craft with your kids. On your weaker days, you'll be glad you did.

Garbage in, garbage out. This is an age-old law, one that has proven true over and over again. Whatever we expose ourselves to will eventually bear fruit in our lives (be it good or rotten). It is prideful to think we can watch filthy movies, listen to lewd lyrics, or engage in low conversations without being affected by them. This charge is not to promote legalism—quite the opposite. This is a challenge to look around our lives and do some housecleaning for the expressed purpose of pursuing greater health and holiness. There is a big difference between a prideful posture that boasts, "I would NEVER watch such a thing!" and the heart that humbly says, "I just can't watch that. I care about my mind-set, my soul, and my health. Jesus wouldn't want me to be a part of that."

Less is more. You've heard this before, but it is worth repeating: Simplify your life. When we are spread too thin, our stress level goes up, and we lose sight of simple peace and joy. When we are committed to more than we should be, we are at greater risk of falling into temptation, losing perspective of what is important, and of missing the spontaneous voice of God in our lives. Often we become too busy because we have a hard time saying no, we want to impress somebody, we want something God hasn't provided yet, or we simply lack the faith to cut the extras from our lives. Women often struggle with discontentment; this is one of the devil's greatest weapons. Think of Eve in the Garden of Eden. She lived in a perfect place, and yet the devil convinced her she was *entitled to more.* When we think we are entitled to more than God is giving us, we grab stuff for ourselves and cause our lives to become cluttered and out of balance. But as our lives become more focused, less stressed, and more reliant on God, something wonderful happens: We end up having *more.* More energy, more joy, more grace for others, and a better perspective. One of my favorite verses is 1 Timothy 6:6: "But godliness with contentment is great gain" (NIV). Think about it. When we pursue a closer walk with God and respond to His upward call *while* embracing a heart of contentment for *where we are at right now*, we gain. We have much to gain by doing less, doing it better, and waiting on God's timing for our lives.

Say no to yourself on a regular basis. "I beat my body and make it my slave so that after I have preached to others, I myself will not be disqualified for the prize" (1 Corinthians 9:27 NIV). Just because you can afford to buy something, eat something, or do something doesn't always mean you should. Every day, in some small way, say no to yourself. Don't give yourself everything your heart desires; say no and make yourself deal with it. The Bible tells us to *exercise* self-control. That means we must put it into practice. Self-restraint has become unpopular in our world, and yet it is a precious fruit of the Holy Spirit—one that will keep us out of trouble if we stay close to the Lord and apply His principles to our lives.

Understand that continual self-indulgence leads to a drop in standard. "To learn, you must love discipline" (Proverbs 12:1). While we need to treat ourselves once in a while, to do so all the time would allow our indulgences to push us backward. No one is meant to *live* in "party mode," and if that lifestyle is pursued, that person will quickly come to ruin. Take inventory, search your heart, and see if there are any indulgences to which you have become a slave. Little treats here and there bless our days and give us a lift. I'm not talking about those things; I'm talking about the indulgences that have a hold on us. Indulgences we make provision for and become very cranky if life gets in the way of our getting them. Again, please understand. This inventory is not to promote legalism. It is for you to tighten things up in your life so that your time and energy are invested in moving you forward into what God has for you. Ask the Lord to show you if there is an area in your life that needs to be liberated by His power. He will deliver you if you allow Him to.

Take a vision inventory. Once or twice a year, get alone with God for the purpose of waiting, listening, and receiving a fresh vision from Him for your life. Write it down and tuck it in your Bible.

Take a moment now and consider the nourishment you receive through food and the things you are exposed to. Are there steps toward better health and wholeness you could begin to take today? Initially it will take extra effort, but in the long run, you will be strengthened and that strength will carry you. And remember, His mercies are new every morning and His faithfulness is great (see Lamentations 3:21-24).

God in heaven,

You are all I need. Forgive me for the countless times I've looked to the things of this world to satisfy my hunger. Please, Lord, increase my hunger for You. Heighten my sensitivity to Your Spirit so I can sense ahead of time when I am about to choose something that is less than Your best for me. I want my whole life to be nourished by You so that I can be constantly aware of Your presence in my life. Lord Jesus, I want more of You in me. Amen.

Steps Toward Health

- If my eating is completely out of control, I will repent of the imbalance I have allowed in my life. I will be thankful for Christ's forgiveness and His promise to help me.

- If I don't eat too much, but I eat all the wrong things, I will acknowledge that my body is the temple of the Lord. I will ask

God's forgiveness for becoming lazy in my diet. I will seek His help as I make necessary adjustments.

- If I naturally eat well, I will thank the Lord for motivating me to do so. I will pray for the friend who struggles in this area. I will stay humble and not think for a moment that I am exceptional because I eat well. I will remember that pride goes before a fall. God has allowed me to gain victory over this area, and I will in turn intercede for someone else's victory.

TRY THIS

- Don't weigh yourself more than once every two weeks. Put your focus on your health, and eventually your weight will fall into place.

- Don't allow yourself to eat sweets during the week. Treat yourself on the weekends.

- Make yourself eat something for breakfast which includes some kind of protein (eggs, protein shake, peanut butter on whole wheat toast, etc.). You will feel better and be less apt to crash and burn later in the day.

- Buy a cool water bottle and keep yourself hydrated throughout the day.

- When you eat at a fast-food restaurant, choose a salad or grilled meat without the bun.

- Walk away from toxic conversations, movies, and music.

- Tell yourself daily, "I am fearfully and wonderfully made. I am getting stronger and healthier every day!"

Balance Application

As I mentioned earlier, if you are in a good place, use your strength to gain extra ground. Make especially good choices and stick with them. If you are faltering and feeling weak, pray and ask for God's help. Don't give up completely. Just do your best and hold your ground. If you are in crisis mode, you may be forced into going without meals or eating irregularly. This is not the time to worry about your diet. Entrust yourself to your heavenly Father, and your life will adjust accordingly. If you have an addictive background and/or unresolved issues of anger or unforgiveness, this chapter may do little more than get under your skin. The suggestions about not eating for the wrong reasons may cause you to feel defensive and angry. The most important thing for you right now is to get to the bottom of your feelings. The advice in this chapter is not meant to be a substitute for professional counsel, but rather a supplement to it. If this applies to you, I ask you, sister, to please go after wholeness and health. Let nothing deter you. Freedom is waiting for you.

There is a lot of information in this chapter, and you may need to read it a few times. Incorporate one or two of these principles at a time and make them a part of your everyday life. Come back to this chapter every once in a while and take inventory. When you are ready, add another discipline.

Study Time

1. Think about the last time you ate for the wrong reason. What was that reason? How did you feel afterward?

2. Think about the last time you ate far too much. Describe the thoughts that went through your head afterward.

3. Did those thoughts weaken you or strengthen you?

4. Describe at least four ways the overeating incident affected your mental, physical, and spiritual health.

5. When you take a step back and look at how too much food actually weakens you on many levels, do you feel inspired or overwhelmed at the thought of taking some healthy steps? Share this with a friend and ask for accountability.

6. Read Romans 5:1-5. What makes us right in God's sight? What allows us to stand in that highest place of privilege? Describe what those things mean to you.

7. What are the by-products of our faith?

8. Read verses 3-5 again. Why does He allow us to struggle?

9. Read and meditate on this beautiful passage one more time, slowly. Ask the Holy Spirit to fill your heart with God's love today.

Six

Get Your Body to Work as It Should

I discipline my body like an athlete, training it to do what it should. Otherwise, I fear that after preaching to others I myself might be disqualified.

1 Corinthians 9:27

I SETTLED BACK IN MY SEAT, BUCKLED MY SEAT BELT, and pulled out my notebook. I had a three-hour flight and was thankful for the extra time to study. At the time I was a fitness trainer, and my notes were opened to anatomy and physiology. I was lost in the material until I sensed the man sitting next to me peering over my shoulder. I looked over at him, smiled, and asked, "How are you doing today?"

He smiled back and said, "Fitness, huh?"

"Yes, sir," I replied.

Right away he told me his story. "One day my wife was doing the dishes and something outside caught her attention. She looked out the window, then at me, and said, 'Wow. That Bob is really in good shape.' I looked out the window to see our muscle-bound neighbor running by." My seatmate became more animated as he continued.

"So I puffed up my chest, pulled in my gut, looked at my wife, and said, 'I can do that,' and within minutes I was in my workout clothes and outside running. I ran seven miles."

"What happened?"

His shoulders dropped as he sighed. "I damaged my Achilles tendons and now I can barely walk straight. So what'd I do wrong?"

I could tell this guy could take some teasing, so I said, "You let your ego get the best of you!"

He sat back in his seat and said, "I know. I really blew it. I used to be in great shape, and I compared the guy I used to be to my bodybuilder neighbor. Now I can't run at all."

I encouraged the man to remember the more important things in life, like loving his wife and being defined by who he is and not by what he produces. We had a great talk, and afterward he seemed to feel better.

I share this story because it is a perfect example of what happens to people every single day. We cannot compare ourselves to who we were years ago, nor can we compare ourselves to others. Those kinds of evaluations produce no good results.

Little Steps in the Right Direction

The only way to gain ground in the area of physical fitness is to honestly assess:

- Where am I at right now?
- What are my limitations?
- Where would I like to be?
- How do I get there?

Once we honestly answer these questions, we are facing the right direction and ready to get started. I cannot tell you how many times I was in excellent shape only to get injured, have a crisis, or be put on bed rest for pregnancy. Each time I reentered the ring, I was practically starting over. My first few trips back to the club were so defeating because I knew in my head how to take fitness to the next level, and yet my body was weak and needed to be treated like a beginner. Once I got a hold of that fact, I decided to embrace the challenge as an opportunity to grow in humility, patience, focus, and discipline. I wrapped my arms around the struggle and gave myself permission to take one step at a time toward getting fit again.

The human body is so divinely wired that you can get it to do almost anything...as long as you ask it nicely. In other words, you— yes, you—are capable of doing the splits, running in a race, or doing push-ups (unless you've got a disability; although thousands with disabilities find ways around their disability to achieve a greater level of health). To get your body to do something that seems beyond you, you must introduce the idea by taking little steps in that direction.

Over time, your body will not only respond to your requests, it will help you get to where you are going. For instance, if your goal is to increase your flexibility (which is an excellent idea for any-body), begin by stretching your muscles gently (after you've done a proper warm-up). Do not bounce or push yourself too far. If you keep this up and each day stretch a *little* further, eventually your body learns that it's okay to stretch that far and adapts to what you are asking it to do. Before you know it, you've significantly increased your range of motion and eliminated many of your aches and pains. Isn't that amazing?

It's the same with running. As you gradually introduce your body to the idea of this kind of exertion, your body will read the consistent messages you are sending and eventually "help you out" by being more efficient with oxygen supply, heart/lung support, and recovery. Running is not for everybody, but every person is wired and made for some form of cardio exercise. Believe it or not, eventually your cardio exercise will grow easier and you will begin to feel better than you ever have before. The key is to take small steps, give consistent messages, and be patient with yourself. In our spiritual lives the Bible tells us to run with patient endurance (Hebrews 12:1). *Running* with *patience* sounds like an oxymoron, and yet it is the patient runner who finishes strong. Proverbs 4:12 says, "If you live a life guided by wisdom, you won't limp or stumble as you run." Exercise wisdom as you gradually introduce your body to this kind of exercise, and you will go far.

There is an old adage in fitness that says, "Take more ground on the good days." You know those days when you wake up and, for some reason, you just feel great? You have energy and focus, and you feel motivated. It is tempting to retrace your steps and ask, "Okay, what did I do right yesterday? What did I eat? How much sleep did I get?" and so on. Well, many trainers will tell you to go the extra mile on those days. Run farther, lift more, push harder. Take advantage of the strong days and gain more ground. This will compensate for those days when you do less.

I am going to use this theme throughout the rest of the book in dealing with both our physical and our spiritual health. One of our goals is to understand and embrace when it is healthy to push harder than we are used to and when it is wise to pull back and rest. *At the heart of true, lasting balance is the ability to read your health and your circumstances and then adjust accordingly.* As you gear up to take your fitness to the next level, here are a few things to keep in mind.

Tangible Tips as You Prepare for Exercise

Take an honest assessment. Assess where you are at in your health and in your stage of life. Set realistic goals and make a plan that works for you. Do you work out better alone or with someone? Is it easier on your family if you exercise in the morning or at night? Know that God has created you to move, and He will honor your desire for a healthy body as long as you keep that desire balanced with other priorities.

Ask nicely. Be content to start where you need to. Resist the temptation to look around at where anyone else is in their pursuit of health and fitness. Walk, lift, or stretch just beyond what is comfortable for you (more on this later).

Leave your comfort zone. In order to grow, we must continually push beyond what is comfortable. Once you have assessed your ability, continually ask your body to do a *little bit* more. You will notice as you push just beyond what is "normal" for you that your threshold will increase, and you will begin to gain ground in the area you are working. Ronald E. Osborn wrote, "Undertake something that is difficult; it will do you good. Unless you try to do something beyond what you have already mastered, you will never grow."

Don't give up what you've gained. It is much harder to get something back than it is to maintain it. Think about relationships, good habits, and skills. In every area of life, there are examples of things that require our attention or we eventually lose them. Exerting a little bit of effort now is far easier than dealing with the consequences later. Keep that piece of wisdom in your mind when looking at exercise (and at life). Truly, you only need to exercise about three to four hours per week to enjoy great health. Some will work out more, others less; but four hours out of 168 is a small investment for the great returns you will enjoy.

Understand atrophy. To further clarify the previous point, when we allow our good habits to get away from us, breakdown happens. Atrophy basically means breaking down or wasting away. Our muscles atrophy when we stop exercising either by choice or by illness or injury. Because of this, too much time in bed after an injury, surgery, or illness is no longer advised. Doctors, nurses, and therapists are encouraging patients to get up and get going so the healing process can continue and so your muscles won't waste away. If you experience a setback in exercise, it may seem that your gains come slower than your losses, but even so, press on.

Take more ground on the good days. This was mentioned already, but it must be at the forefront of your mind in order to continue forward movement. Try it. On your good days, push a little harder; you will feel exhilarated by the challenge. You will also get a glimpse of your potential.

It takes energy to make energy. Just as it takes money to make money, it takes energy to make energy. Often people will tell me that they don't exercise because they don't have the energy. With the exception of some underlying disease, exercise is the remedy for a person with low energy. For several years after my battle with a disease, I struggled with fatigue. I was also an aerobics instructor at the time. I cannot tell you how many nights I was scheduled to teach and yet felt overwhelmed with exhaustion. I knew I had to show up to teach my class, so I pulled myself up by my bootstraps and got myself to the club.

I can honestly say that for every single time I taught a class in spite of sheer exhaustion, 95 percent of the time I left feeling great. It was only in the cases where I was on the verge of a cold or flu that the exercise made me even more tired. Just try it. Invest a little energy on those tired days and see if you don't get positive results. It is important to note that when you first start out with exercising, you *will* feel more fatigued after exercise until you get used to it. In fact, how you recover is a good measuring tool for how you are progressing in your overall fitness.

Listen to your body. This may seem in conflict with my previous point, but read on. Another reason we should take small steps at a time is so we can pay attention to how our body is responding. Some days we will respond beautifully, and other days we will feel a bit rough afterward. One day at the end of an aerobics class, we were taking our recovery heart rate. I noticed a perplexed look on one of my regular attendees. I asked her if she was okay. She replied, "I feel fine. I felt great during class, and yet I am not recovering as efficiently as I usually do." I encouraged her to walk around a bit more, drink water, stay out of the sauna, and pay attention to how she was feeling. She wasn't in class the following week, and she told me later that she got the stomach flu that evening. She didn't feel it coming, but already her body was responding differently to exercise. The point is that once you get into a groove and are used to your workout program, it is easy to go on autopilot and not pay attention to how your body is responding. If you are sweating more than usual, if your heart rate goes up too fast, or you just don't feel the same, back off a bit, drink your water, and listen to your body.

Don't go through the motions. I used to teach an advanced-level step class. I was always intrigued by the various levels of workouts taking place in the same studio with the same choreography. Some of my members would be soaked in sweat, breathing hard, using full range of motion, and yipping and hollering when things got really intense. Others would stay very close to their step, hardly move their limbs, and were barely sweating and breathing. I always told my members to listen to their bodies and work at their own pace. I love it when people feel secure enough to take care of themselves during their workouts. But I have also seen others get frustrated with their lack of progress, even though they were barely putting anything into their exercise. When you understand body mechanics, you will be able to get an intense workout doing the most basic of moves. For now, just remember to be fully present when you are exercising.

Throw yourself into what you are doing. If you are walking, swing your arms; make every move count and pay attention to your body when something hurts. Another reason not to go through the motions is so we don't overlook this very important fact: If we are healthy enough to exercise, we are blessed indeed. May we never take that for granted. Just as food tastes much better when we are fully present and fully aware of how blessed we are, exercise feels like a breath of fresh air when we embrace every opportunity to exercise as a gift from God.

Precious Lord,

Thank You for the gift of my body. I will say this every day in spite of the many flaws I see. You have gifted me with a measure of health, and I will use it for Your glory. I want to take care of the good things I have been given so I can give You a great return on Your investment in me. As I pursue a greater level of physical health, keep me close to Your heartbeat. I want to keep things in perspective, and I want to honor You in everything I do. Thank You for loving me the way You do. I love You too. Amen.

Steps Toward Health

- I will take an honest assessment of my current fitness level.

- I will write down some tangible, doable goals to be accomplished over the next four weeks.

- I will resist the temptation to compare myself with others, or even with a level of fitness I was at years ago.

- When I am tempted not to work out, I will call a friend and ask her to walk with me.

- I will not entertain thoughts that weaken or defeat me. I will put my hope in the Lord.

TRY THIS

- Get a physical. Let your doctor know about your exercise plans and follow his or her advice.

- Decide what kind of exercise you want to do and invest in a good pair of shoes appropriate for that activity. The right shoes are *extremely important* for protecting your joints.

- Here's an easy way to keep track of your exercise. Put a small *o* on your calendar on the days you get cardio exercise; put a small *x* on the days you do strength work. This will help keep you accountable and also give you a realistic perspective of how often you are exercising. Typically, it is good to do strength work two to three times per week, and cardio exercise three to five times per week. For some, this may feel like a lofty goal. Always remember, something is better than nothing.

- If you cannot afford a club membership, consider renting a piece of equipment for your home. Some places will allow you to rent-to-own. When my kids were very young, I rented a treadmill during the winter months and exercised while they were napping.

- If renting a piece of equipment is out of the question, consider purchasing a couple of exercise videos or seeing if your local library checks some out. One of the videos should give you more than 20 minutes of cardio (aerobic exercise), and the other one should work your muscles. Make sure these videos give more than a couple minutes to stretching at the end of your workout. While I am sure there are countless good videos out there, try to purchase videos that are instructed by someone who holds a certification in fitness. Just because someone is famous doesn't mean they know a lot about proper body mechanics. There may be several new instructors who have recently hit the scene that I don't know about, but let me suggest a few instructors I do know about and who are true experts in the field: Kathy Smith, Gin Miller, Karen Voight, and Kari Anderson. These women know what they are talking about, and anything you would purchase by them would be thorough and give you a safe workout.*

Balance Application

Part of moving forward is taking an honest assessment of where we are now. There is no shame in this at all. In fact, it takes courage and humility to admit where we are, what we need, and where we want to go. As long as we are in Christ, we can admit our weakness and need, and then we can look up to find our strength in Him. Even in our weakness, especially in our weakness, we say out loud, "But my God is strong in me." The Lord cares about our health and wants us to be free and victorious in every area of our lives. This is my prayer for you: "Dear friend, I pray that you may prosper in every way and be in good health, just as your soul prospers" (3 John 1:2 HCSB).

---

* I have not viewed all of their videos and therefore am not aware of music or choreography that may or may not be acceptable to you.

Study Time

1. Read Proverbs 16:32.

2. What are the two key virtues this verse speaks of?

3. Write this verse down in your own words, applying it to your own situation. (For example, "It's better for me to...")

4. Once more, write this verse down, but this time in prayer form. (For example, "Lord, I will be...")

5. Read Proverbs 25:28. Apply this verse to your own life. In what ways could your life be toppled without self-control?

6. Read 2 Peter 1:6.

7. Do we have enough strength in ourselves to make lasting changes in our lives? Explain.

8. To grow physically and spiritually, we need self-control, patient endurance, and godliness. What leads us to these things?

9. How do you get to know someone better?

10. What will you do differently this week?

Seven

Time to Move!

*For I can do everything with the help of Christ
who gives me the strength I need.*

PHILIPPIANS 4:13

RECENTLY I ASKED OUR FAMILY DOCTOR, "What would you say is the most prevailing problem among your patients?" Without hesitating he said, "A sedentary lifestyle. Most of my patients would not need to be seen if they simply ate less and exercised more." That day as I drove home, I pondered my doctor's words. My thoughts were interrupted when the radio blared with a new report from the Center for Disease Control. Did you know that each year in the United States, as many as 300,000 people die from obesity-related issues? More and more we are hearing that this issue has reached epidemic proportions and is now affecting our children.

Exercise is important for our health, our outlook, and our quality of life. Physical imbalance is a serious problem, and yet the remedy is simple: We need to eat better, eat less, and get moving. As I mentioned earlier, it takes energy to make energy, but the payoff is worth it.

As we prepare to improve our lifestyle, we must also prepare ahead for those days in which it would be easier to do nothing. It is easier to eat what is in front of us rather than put the time into preparing something healthy. It is easier to sit on the couch in front of the TV after a long, hard day, but we all know that the easier path is rarely the fruitful path. The Bible says, "The slacker craves, yet has nothing, but the diligent is *fully satisfied*" (Proverbs 13:4 HCSB, emphasis added). Here are a few tips to help you prepare ahead of time for those days when you just don't feel like exercising:

- Write down your goals in a simple form and put them on your refrigerator.
- Exercise with a friend. Your chances of canceling your workout are reduced by about 50 percent.
- Make provision in your schedule for your workout ahead of time. When you go through your day *in the hope* that time won't get away from you, know that it will every time.

Okay, so here we go. We've talked about physical "input"—how we nourish ourselves. Now we move on to "output"—how we respond to what's been deposited in us. We are wired to move, and the more we move, the more efficiently our body responds to what we are asking it to do. This chapter is filled with practical and technical advice on exercise. Don't allow yourself to become overwhelmed. Just digest a little at a time. This is good information for you to have. Knowing and applying proper technique will allow you the best results possible.

There are five components to fitness:

1. Cardio/respiratory endurance
2. Muscular strength
3. Muscular endurance
4. Flexibility
5. Body composition

To keep things simple and basic, we will talk about three of them:

1. Cardio/respiratory endurance
2. Strength work (referring to both muscular strength and endurance)
3. Flexibility

Cardio/Respiratory Endurance

Cardio/respiratory endurance is measured by how our heart and lungs respond to movement. There are three things that affect our cardio endurance: how often we exercise, how intensely we exercise, and how long each workout lasts. Every day that we set aside time for the specific purpose of getting our hearts pumping and filling our lungs with oxygen for a sustained period of time, we give our body the gift of these benefits:

1. Balanced "input"
2. Increased circulation
3. Strengthened heart and lung systems
4. Improved organ function
5. Improved outlook
6. Metabolized fat
7. Reduced stress
8. Improved appearance and sense of health and strength

As I have traveled around and spoken to women, I've been asked this question many times, "I'm a mom of several children. I run after them all day long...isn't *that* exercise? And if so, why am I not losing weight?" This is an excellent question. There are two forms of cardio exercise: aerobic and anaerobic. *Aerobic* basically means "in the presence of oxygen" and *anaerobic* means "without the presence of oxygen."

You may ask, "But aren't we living, breathing creatures? Aren't we always using oxygen to live?" Yes, this is true. As you sit and read this book, your body is at a certain level of *homeostasis,* meaning your input of oxygen and the demand you are placing on your body are in balance with each other. But if you were to get up and run up the stairs, your heart would start pumping, requiring an energy system to kick in. In this case your body would use the anaerobic energy system because your run upstairs required quick, accessible energy. Your body stores a certain amount of energy in your muscles that is ready and available for quick movement. You may have recently eaten some carbohydrates, and your body has broken them down and stored them for when you will need them for quick use.

"Quick use" might mean running across the mall parking lot in the rain, rushing to the edge of your yard to keep your toddler from running into the street, or simply running after your children throughout the day. Because these activities require only stints of energy, your body uses up the carbohydrates stored in your muscles. An important note here: This is often why we get the munchies throughout the day. Our bodies want us to replenish those immediate energy stores. Where we go wrong is munching on empty calories that do little more than raise our blood sugar level to high buzz, only to allow us to crash and burn a little later in the day. This is why I love a healthy snack bar. It provides protein, vitamins, and carbohydrates.

There is a great purpose for the anaerobic energy system. As you can see, there are countless scenarios each day that require quick movement. When you pick up around the house (low level of energy expended) and when you sprint across the parking lot (high level of energy expended for a short time), you will tap into your anaerobic system. There are many sports that are anaerobic in nature, like gymnastics, golf, short sprints in track-and-field, etc. Athletes who train in the anaerobic zone increase their threshold and their bodies recover much more efficiently than those who are not used to that kind of exercise.

I am writing to the average person who is not a trained athlete. In order to burn fat, work out longer, and recover in a more enjoyable fashion, you need to work out in the aerobic zone. In other words, you need a nice, slow warm-up that sends your body the message, "I am warming up slowly. I am going to be out here for a while, and I need oxygen to help me." Just a note about the warm-up. When we start working out too quickly without a proper warm-up, we are telling our bodies, "There is no way I can possibly sustain this pace for a long period of time so I probably won't need any oxygen." Our nervous system reads that message and suddenly we find ourselves breathing hard, needing to slow way down, and wondering if we are even cut out for this exercise thing.

Once you begin a nice, slow warm-up, you will feel your heart rate gradually increase. Give yourself time to get used to the increase and little by little increase your intensity until you are breathing hard but can still carry on a conversation. You will notice when you hit the "zone" that you will have arrived at a new level of balance or homeostasis. In other words, the demand you are putting on your body is met with the necessary oxygen to fulfill the task. Isn't that amazing?

This is where it gets fun. It takes about 20 minutes of this kind of sustained exercise to efficiently burn fat. That's why you want to work toward a cardio workout of about 45 minutes. This is not a hard and fast rule, but more of a generic scale. Each person is different, and each of us will access oxygen either quickly or slowly, depending on our current fitness level. The more fit you are, the quicker you will be able to warm up, access oxygen, and recover afterward. When you take the time to invest in your health, your body pays you back in great dividends.

Here are a few things to remember:

1. Exercise on an empty stomach or after a light snack.
2. Drink plenty of water before, during (if possible), and after exercise. Muscles work better when they are hydrated, and drinking water is like "internal" exercise.
3. Give yourself five to seven minutes to warm up.
4. Listen to your body and push just beyond what you feel like doing.
5. Give yourself five to ten minutes to cool down.
6. *Always* gently stretch after exercise.

Strength Work

Muscular strength refers to the amount of weight you are able to lift. *Muscular endurance* refers to how many repetitions you are able to complete. To keep it simple, muscular strength asks "how much" and muscular endurance asks "how long." When we regularly invest some of our time building strong, lean muscles, these are the benefits we enjoy:

1. Supported frame
2. Minimized risk of injury
3. Increased circulation
4. Improved outlook
5. Increased levels of strength
6. Increased metabolism (which helps us burn fat more efficiently)

7. Increased physical freedom

8. Improved appearance and sense of health and strength

A point to remember...*heavy things either injure us or make us stronger.* Every single day someone is injured from either lifting improperly or moving an object that is too heavy for them. Proper strength work strengthens our frame and lessens our chance of injury. Strength work consists of exercises that tone your muscles. You can use weights or your own body weight as a form of resistance. As we regularly engage in physical resistance training, our strength limitations are broken down and a new threshold is built back up, giving us an increased capacity for lifting, pushing, and pulling.

In order to grow, we have to push beyond what is comfortable, which requires effort and energy. That is why it is important to give our muscle groups a day of recovery after working them. Proper technique is also of paramount importance. The slightest rotation of a body part could make all the difference between working the muscle and injuring the joint. That is why you want to seek instruction from one who knows about proper alignment.

As I mentioned earlier, the instructors on the videos I suggested spend a lot of time cuing proper body alignment. Also, if you belong to a reputable health club, the personal trainers there should be able to walk you through a list of good strength exercises and proper form. As you stay consistent with your strength work, you will carry yourself differently, you will feel better, and you will enjoy more physical freedom.

Building muscle, as I mentioned above, will also change your metabolism. That's right; you can change your metabolism! If you have a slow metabolism, engage in a thorough and safe strength work routine about two to four times per week, and you will enjoy noticeable changes in no time. A fitness friend recently told me that if you build two pounds of muscle into your frame, you will burn 13 more pounds of fat per year. As your muscle density increases, so will your metabolism.

Flexibility

Flexibility is determined by the range of motion you have around each joint. This is probably the most neglected component of exercise. Many people are vigorous in their cardio and strength workouts, only to skip stretching afterward. People have told me that stretching takes too much time. You can get away with this for a while, but eventually muscles (especially developing ones) will get tighter and tighter, becoming a recipe for injury. Most injuries require a time of rest, which sets you back to where you started from. So invest some time stretching. It is essential.

When you stretch, avoid bouncing. Make sure your stretches are gentle and deliberate. If you ask your body to stretch too far too soon, your muscles will rebound and you may injure yourself. As with every other component of fitness, take small, consistent steps. I deal with a lot of regular pain due to my problematic joint issues. I have learned that every time my body begins to ache, I need to spend some extra time stretching. I would venture to say that most of our aches and pains would be eliminated if we stretched regularly. Here are a few things to remember:

- *Don't stretch cold muscles.* It is better to do a thorough stretch at the end of your workout. However, doing basic range of motion movements without a workout is better than not doing them at all. Just do not stretch cold muscles too deeply.

- *Don't hold your breath when stretching.* Keep your breathing steady. Breathe in through the nose and out through the mouth.

* *Hold your stretches for 10-20 seconds.* If your muscle starts to rebound or pull back, release the stretch and next time don't pull quite as far.

Tangible Tips for Exercise

Choose your workout days. Talk to family members and decide which days you will work out each week. It is much easier to stay consistent if your schedule doesn't vary too much.

Choose your cardio mode. It doesn't matter whether you are walking, running, taking an aerobics class, or following an exercise video. Just have your plan ahead of time and stick to it. (The "I'll figure it out when I get there" mind-set is never very effective.)

Balance your strength work. It is best to work opposing muscle groups in the same workout. Most aerobics classes and videos are designed this way. If you are working out on your own, think of it this way: If you work biceps, work your triceps; if you work your chest, work your back; if you work your quadriceps (upper thigh), work your hamstrings (back upper leg). Working opposing muscle groups will keep you balanced and strong. If you ever see a muscle-bound body builder who hovers over his bulging pectoral (chest) muscles, know that he most likely has not done enough back work or proper stretching. We can actually pull our bodies out of alignment if we work one muscle group without working the other.

Change things up every once in a while. Because our bodies are so adaptable, they will adjust to the consistent messages we send them. This works in our favor for a while because our systems become more efficient. Where this can work against us, though, is when we hit a plateau. If we fall into the rut of doing the same thing all the time, we cease to be challenged and need to introduce something new into our routine. This is why cross training is so effective. Challenge your system by throwing in a different mode of exercise. You can also change your usual workout by increasing the intensity or length of your workout. This will give your body an athletic edge and keep you from falling into a rut.

Make time for stretching. This bears repeating: Set aside a little time for stretching. You will feel wonderful afterward, and you will greatly reduce your risk of injury. Even ten minutes at the end of your workout—which adds up to only 40 minutes per week—will literally change how you feel and how you respond to exercise.

Don't make decisions while running uphill. I learned this the hard way, but it is a good one. Whether you are literally at the hard part in your workout, a hard part of your day, or even struggling in a difficult time in life, don't decide what your goals are (or aren't) or how far you will be able to go (or not). Wait until you level out and you are breathing regularly before you honestly assess where things are with you.

Know that your disciplines will carry you—for a while. But only for a while. Once you get into a groove, your body will get better and better at responding to what you are asking it to do. What is wonderful is that you can have an off day or two and step out of your routine while still enjoying the benefits of your past disciplines. But this will only go so far. If your "off days" become the rule rather than the exception, your body will then begin to read those messages and respond accordingly. So do your best not to let your diet and exercise routine get away from you by more than a few days. Again remember, if you are in a short-term crisis, exercise will be the furthest thing from your mind. If you are in a long-term crisis, you will *need* to keep your strength up by taking care of yourself. It is one of the smartest things you can do.

For some, the whole diet and exercise thing may seem way out of reach. If you feel this way, try the following easy steps which may help you change the momentum in your life.

Ten Steps in Ten Weeks to Tiptoe Toward a Healthy Lifestyle

Add one discipline at a time while continuing the previous ones.

- Week one: Drink eight to ten glasses of water daily.

- Week two: Add one fruit a day to your diet.

- Week three: Commit to ten minutes of exercise two to four times this week (for example, stretch, walk, do sit-ups, etc.).

- Week four: Rid yourself of a bad habit—and work to keep it out of your life. (Remember, maintenance is easier than gaining lost ground.)

- Week five: Add one vegetable a day to your diet.

- Week six: Increase the length of your workout by ten to fifteen minutes.

- Week seven: Add another fruit to your diet.

- Week eight: Change your "indulgence" rule. Whether you overindulge in sweets, breads, or fried foods, make yourself abide by a more disciplined rule (for example, limit sweets or fried foods to weekends only).

- Week nine: Quit eating after dinner and before bed (or at least change the rule to weekends only).

- Week ten: Assess your progress and make any necessary adjustments (for example, if you are still eating too much or not exercising enough, do your best to bring balance in these areas).

Dear Lord,

I am thankful that nothing is too hard for You, not even getting me on a schedule. I will look to You each day for strength, wisdom, and protection as I seek a more balanced and disciplined life. Help me to know when it is wise to push through the obstacles and when You are calling me to pull back a bit. You are my goal, not a perfectly fit body, so I will keep my eyes on You, knowing You will lead me in the way that I should go. You understand me and my stage of life, and You love me. Help me to listen to everything You say to me. Amen.

Steps Toward Health

- I will thank God out loud for the many gifts He has given me.
- I will put some time into exercise today.
- I will call a good friend and ask her to keep me accountable.
- I will push myself just beyond my comfort zone.

TRY THIS

- Set a goal to work out several times per week for the next month. If you achieve this goal, treat yourself to something special. This can be very motivating!

- As you get used to your workouts, put more energy into your movements. Notice how easy it is to increase your intensity.

- When you feel unmotivated, go over your fitness goals and make yourself do *something*.

- Use a towel for the stretching portion of your workout. Lie on your back and hold the ends of the towel in your hands. Straighten one of your legs and put the arch of that foot in the loop of the towel. Gently pull on the ends of the towel so that your leg comes towards you. This is a safe and effective way to stretch your hamstrings.

* Improve your posture. Whether you are sitting down or standing up, make a conscious effort to sit up straight. Pull your shoulders back and your abs in. This simple habit engages muscles that help support your frame. Plus, it takes pounds off of your appearance.

Balance Application

At first this information may seem overwhelming, but in time it will become second nature. As you do the exercises, you will begin to notice when something doesn't feel right. Pay attention to how you are feeling. If you are struggling because it is difficult, that's okay; make yourself exercise anyway. But if a certain joint feels unstable or you are experiencing unusual pain, then be sure and stop and talk to your doctor. Usually when someone buys an expensive piece of equipment, they take the time to read the manual so that they can get the best use and so as not to damage the equipment by their lack of knowledge. As you learn the basic mechanics of movement, you will be able to do effective strength work in your living room, your hotel room, or even out on your deck. Give yourself room to grow and learn, and you will experience the great satisfaction of having a healthy, strong body.

Study Time

1. Read 1 Corinthians 9:26-27.

2. What are the ways God is calling you to discipline your body?

3. What steps will you take to move in that direction?

4. Does the thought of incorporating a regular exercise program intimidate or overwhelm you?

5. Read Philippians 4:13. Read it again and meditate on this promise.

6. Write out a personalized prayer of faith incorporating this verse.

7. Read 1 Timothy 4:8.

8. What is far more important than exercising our physical body?

9. What kind of season are you in with the Lord right now?

10. Pause and ask the Lord to draw you deeper with Him. Pray for your loved ones.

Eight

Too Busy to Rest?

It's useless to rise early and go to bed late,
and work your worried fingers to the bone.
Don't you know he enjoys giving rest to those
he loves?

PSALM 127:2 MSG

I REMEMBER A TIME WHEN MY SONS WERE BABIES. I was fighting a disease and trying to keep it all together. For the first three years of his life, my youngest child got up every other hour. I received all kinds of advice on getting him to sleep, and none of it worked. Added to my lack of consistent sleep were a toddler and a preschooler who *had* gotten a good night's sleep. They were ready to party at the break of dawn! One more factor that complicated things immensely was the illness I was battling. Lyme disease stole every ounce of energy I had. I experienced countless scary neurological symptoms while trying to care for my three little ones. My poor husband worked two jobs and spent every free moment caring for our busy household. He carried a weight of worry for our finances, my health, and our future. By the time his head hit the pillow at night, he was snoring. Most nights I tried to let him get his much-needed rest.

One night as I lay in bed, desperate for rest, I started to doze into a slumber. My whole body felt as if it were falling into a hole that pulled me from my senses. Oh, how I needed this! I was about to give in to the force that was drawing me into a deeper sleep when I heard a beep, beep, beep. It was the middle of the night, and I thought, *Who would set their alarm and ruin my life this way?* (Thoughts of a desperate woman…) My head seemed to weigh a hundred pounds as I lifted it off the pillow and looked for the alarm. I realized in seconds that it wasn't an alarm; it was my little baby crying again at the top of his lungs. He was sick and coughing up a storm. I dragged my heavy limbs out of bed and into his bedroom. Truly, if a heart could stop beating from sheer exhaustion, I knew mine would. I have never known such fatigue as I did back then.

My kids are older now, and I have more time to rest and recover. As I minister to young moms and look back on my own life, there is another factor that occurs to me. Often, because of our society's mixed-up values, young moms are made to feel incidental. In other words, there are countless messages telling them that it is not enough to put their time into *just* raising their children.

Because we live in a society that constantly measures value by what is achieved or produced, many young moms feel the pressure to be involved in far too many things. I was once one of those young, overcommitted moms; now I am older and deeply burdened for moms who are distracted, depleted, and completely exhausted.

If anyone ever had an excuse or reasons to only do one thing at church, it is a young mother. If anyone has a need for physical and mental rest, it is a young mother. How different it would be for a young mom if she decided to use what little extra time she had to get replenished again. At times that could mean a nap. Other times it could mean a bubble bath, going out to eat, or going to bed early one night. I know and understand the need for some to have something outside the home. To many of us, that sort of thing is a saving grace (but there is a difference between doing *some*thing and five things). I even understand the desire to have a lot of girlfriend connection during this stage of life; one can only talk to toddlers about potty chairs and sippy cups for so long. But still, I would venture to say that young moms would feel better if they put a higher priority on getting the rest their bodies so desperately need.

Rest Is Hard to Come By

This problem doesn't stop with young moms. Women in all seasons of life are juggling countless responsibilities and busy schedules. My mother and my mother-in-law are both retired, and they are as busy as anyone else I know. It seems that our culture just lends itself to this kind of lifestyle. Our fast-paced society puts such a low value on rest and recovery that some think it's only for the weak. The truth of the matter is that rest is *as big* a component to health and fitness as diet and exercise. Since God calls us—even commands us—to rest, He will provide a way for us. Here are a few of the many side effects of a life without rest:

- Weakened immune system
- Loss of perspective
- The healing process is interrupted
- Injuries are more prevalent
- Increased mental strain
- Increased risk of error, misjudgment, mistake, etc.
- Increased strain on relationships
- Balance cannot happen

Chiropractor Dr. Jim Abeler spoke to me about the issue of rest. He said that the majority of his patients who struggle with chronic fatigue syndrome and fibromyalgia have a common thread issue in their lives: interrupted, inconsistent sleep. Whether it is from living near an airport, sleeping next to a snoring husband, or getting up with a baby, these women are exhausted. However, their health would greatly improve if they could get a consistent night's sleep.

Dr. Abeler explained the sleep cycle to me, which was fascinating. Did you know that our bodies supply a necessary growth hormone *only* when we hit that fourth stage of the sleep cycle, and we should typically go through this cycle about three to four times every night? He further explained, "This hormone provides our bodies with something like 'little wrenches.' We need these to build us back up because every day we injure ourselves (daily wear and tear) and every night we need to heal. When our bodies don't get the benefits of that fourth stage of sleep, our health breaks down."

How can we go against the flow of the insane pace of this world and provide ourselves with consistent rest? First, we need to let go of the lie that says, "Rest is an optional, moveable component in my life" and replace it with the truth that says, "Rest replenishes my body and helps me feel my best. God calls me to rest in whatever season I am in, and He will help me find it."

Just as we need to eat better and exercise more efficiently, we need to make sure we get rest. That may sound silly, especially to young moms, but there is both scientific and biblical proof that rest must not be optional. Your efforts may be inconsistent at best, but making rest a high priority in your life will help you do more than just survive a demanding schedule. A heart at rest brings peace to the home. There is no virtue in being worn out all of the time.

This gets at the core of what we believe. If we *really* believe that when we eat better and exercise consistently we will feel better, have more energy, enjoy a higher quality of life, and rid ourselves of the distraction of physical imbalance…if we really believe our choices will make that much of a difference, we will apply ourselves to those things.

Many of us could put a higher value on our need for healthy diet, exercise, and rest and then find a way to work those things into our lives. Millions already do every single day. I've heard stories of people committed to staying healthy and fit and yet too poor for a club membership or even exercise equipment. They didn't let a lack of finances stop them. They filled milk jugs with sand and used them for weights. They rigged pulleys in their basements and created their own equipment. They believed that the benefits of these choices outweighed their many legitimate excuses, and they *found a way*. It's the same with rest. When you start to notice how your perspective improves, how your joy returns, and how much better food energizes you when you are rested, you will protect your need for rest because you will come to believe God when He says that rest will bless you.

Pay Attention to What You Really Need

I woke up one Saturday morning and went through my morning routine. I tried to psych myself up for the long list of chores with my name on them. For some reason I just couldn't get my day off the ground. I was exhausted and lacked the peace and clarity I usually enjoy. My boys were all gone for the day, so I found my way up to my bedroom and turned on the TV. I was just going to watch for a *little bit* and then I would tackle the mountain of laundry that awaited me.

Before I knew what hit me, I realized I had wasted four and half hours watching movies! I peeled myself out of my bed and went downstairs to a pile of dishes in the sink, wrappers on the counter, and my laundry still sitting there. On top of it all, that unsettled feeling in my soul was still with me. I was so mad at myself. I had squandered a perfectly good afternoon. Later that evening I went to the living room to pray. I asked the Lord for forgiveness for wasting the day and spent time with Him until He showed me what was really bothering me.

I lacked peace that morning because I had let my mind wander back to old worries and anxious thoughts. Instead of confessing my fears and replacing them with God's truth, I stuffed them down below the surface. Those unresolved fears hung heavy in my soul that morning and kept me from true joy. Instead of immediately finding my rightful place of peace with God, I found my way up to my bed and laid mindlessly in front of the TV—which did nothing for me. I sat in my living room realizing I lost my peace because I lost sight of Him. So I bowed my head and focused once again on His immeasurable love for me. I got right with Him and sensed His forgiveness, direction, and a fresh dose of mercy.

Well, months later, a similar but different situation occurred. I was coming off of an intense speaking engagement. My family welcomed me home and we enjoyed connecting with one another again. I unpacked, did the laundry, and caught up on things around the house. The following day was Sunday, and after church all of my steam left me. I was absolutely exhausted. I sat down and prayed, "I'm tired, Lord." He so clearly and sweetly said to me, *Go lay down and watch a movie.*

You might find this odd, as did I. My boys were gone for the afternoon, and Kevin was busy in the den, so I snuggled in bed with a book and the remote. I watched the news and read a book during the commercials. I thoroughly enjoyed myself, and when I got up, I felt rested and replenished. What was different this time? I thought through both scenarios and learned a powerful lesson.

God is gracious and gives us room to eat good food, watch fun movies, and spend time doing the things we enjoy. But a critical point must be made here: When we turn to food, movies, and hobbies at times when we *lack peace and intimacy with God*, we are drinking from "cracked cisterns" (Jeremiah 2:13). A cracked cistern is a broken well and is a source far beneath God's best for us.

Read the powerful verse below, but before you do, think about a time when you intentionally chose to medicate yourself with something less than God. Now imagine the surprise of the heavenly hosts, unable to comprehend how any of us could settle for anything less than what has been made available to us.

> Has any nation ever exchanged its gods for another god, even though its gods are nothing? Yet my people have exchanged their glorious God for worthless idols! The heavens are shocked at such a thing and shrink back in horror and dismay, says the LORD. For my people have done two evil things: They have forsaken me—the fountain of living water. And they have dug for themselves cracked cisterns that can hold no water at all! (Jeremiah 2:11-13).

We all choose things over intimacy with Christ. We choose food, shopping, gossip, TV, and so on. We even choose His *gifts* over a love affair with *Him*. And yet He still loves us, still waits patiently for us, and longs for us to understand all we have in Him. The goal here is to abide so closely with the Lord that you *know* when to rest, when to exercise, when to serve, when to pray, and when it's okay just to relax and enjoy the blessings He has given you.

Precious Father,

Thank You for Your gracious love. You have the world on Your shoulders and yet You know how to rest and be at peace. You paid a high price so I could live a life of peace. Help me, Lord, to bring my life into a rhythm that honors You and blesses me. I know there is a way to get the rest I need. Please help me find it. I will look to You to show me the way that I should go, each and every day…and night. I love You, Lord. Amen.

Steps Toward Health

- If I am currently imbalanced in the area of rest, I will pray and ask God to show me what in my life has to change so I can get more rest.

- If I drink too many caffeinated beverages, I will cut back this week.

- If I am involved in too many things, I will write them down, pray about them, talk them over with a trusted friend, and then decide what has to go.

- I will set an honorable timeline for myself to step out of commitments that I know God did not call me to.

- I will determine to honor and protect my God-given call to rest.

TRY THIS

- *Rest from exercise too.* Our need for rest also applies to recovery time from exercise. If you have had an intense workout, give yourself the necessary time to recover. Your organs, your muscles, and your joints all need time to recoup from what you've asked them to do. Listen to your body.

- *Resist the gung ho mentality.* Once you get going on an exercise program, it is easy to get carried away and do too much up front. Pace yourself and give yourself days off in which you don't exercise at all.

- *Routine, routine, routine.* This is essential to living a life with balance, rhythm, and proper rest. Our bodies require a sense of consistency (although, as mentioned earlier, in fitness it is good to break up your routine every once in a while so you don't plateau). Granted, certain stages of life make routine seem like a heroic feat; and that is just what it is. Your body will treat you like a hero if you honor its need for consistency, especially at night. Here are a few suggestions for a bedtime routine:

  - *Read a book at night.* If the news stresses you out, read a heartwarming story.

  - *Drink nighttime tea.* There are many options available. Find one that settles you down without making you feel groggy.

  - *Take a hot bath.* This will soothe your muscles and slow down your heart rate.

  - *Don't lay down more than an hour before bed.* Wait until you are ready to go to sleep, otherwise the quality of your sleep will not be as good.

  - *Stay away from sugar and caffeinated beverages.* At least consider no sugar and/or soda from lunchtime on. This affects sleep for many people.

  - *Guard your mind at night.* Refuse to do what my husband calls "contemplate the universe." Do not let your thoughts wander to things you are worried or anxious about. You can't do anything about them in the middle of the night anyway. Pray yourself to sleep with statements of faith like,

"Lord, I know You care about... Thank You that You are there for me. I give You my concern over... I thank You ahead of time for a good night of rest."

As we wrap up the section on our physical body, let's look at how a life out of balance affects our physical health. Just a note: In the effects listed below, "input" refers mainly to physical nourishment. "Output" refers mainly to physical exercise. "Rest" refers to recovery from exercise, from the demands of life, and mostly to a good night's sleep.

Effects of Physical Imbalance

✓ *Too much input, not enough output:* overweight, lack of energy, increased risk of disease, injury, and depression

✓ *Too much output, not enough input:* undernourished, increased risk of illness and injury, tend to be weak in relationships

   (Important note: Too much input and too much output both result in an increased risk of injury.)

✓ *Too much rest:* atrophy sets in, muscles get soft, strength is swallowed up by weakness

✓ *Too little rest:* weakened immunities, bodily systems breakdown, vulnerable to sickness and disease, loss of perspective, increased risk of injury, loss of strength

   (Important note: Too much rest and too little rest both result in a loss of strength.)

$\mathcal{B}$alance $\mathcal{A}$pplication

Rest is so important. We need to be replenished from exercise, events, busy weeks, and hard conversations. A counselor once told me that it takes our nervous system 48 hours to return to its natural state after a painful conversation. If it takes our divinely wired nervous system a time to recover when pushed beyond its normal boundaries, how much more does our mind, our heart, our joints, and our muscles need to rest and recover from the constant demands of life? We even need to allow our digestive system a time to rest from food. It is important to pay attention to the needs of our body and soul. Rest is a beautiful thing. God-directed rest will replenish and renew us.

Study Time

1. Read the following verse: "My soul finds rest in God alone; my salvation comes from him" (Psalm 62:1 NIV).

2. If we can trust Him with our eternity, we can trust Him with every lesser thing. What thoughts often interrupt your time of rest? Write them down.

3. Look again at what you've written down. Are there any familiar threats, lies, and fears the enemy has used on you before?

4. Read Philippians 4:6-7.

5. Read it again, and again, and again. Memorize it and do what it says.

6. Read Hebrews 4:10-11.

7. According to the Word, what happens in a life without rest? Write it down.

8. Read Jesus' words in Mark 6:31.

9. What ways is He calling you to this place?

10. Will you listen to Him? How?

You are His very precious treasure. Everything you do matters to Him because He loves you.

> Didn't you realize that your body is a sacred place, the place of the Holy Spirit? Don't you see that you can't live however you please, squandering what God paid such a high price for? The physical part of you is not some piece of property belonging to the spiritual part of you. God owns the whole works. So let people see God in and through your body (1 Corinthians 6:19-20 MSG).

Part Two

Spiritual Health

*Physical exercise has some value,
but spiritual exercise is much more important,
for it promises a reward
in both this life and the next.*
1 Timothy 4:8

Nine
God Enjoys You

The glory of God—let it last forever! Let God enjoy his creation!

PSALM 104:31 MSG

I REALLY LIKE MY KIDS. I MEAN, I LOVE THEM intensely, but I also really, really like them. My oldest son, Jake, is in college now, but for many years when he lived at home, he had the most wonderful habit. That boy could not walk by me in the house without wrapping his arm around me, kissing the top of my head, and sweetly saying, "Hi, Mama" or "I love you, Mom." He is passionate and sensitive and, most importantly, he is after the heart of God. He's been a great example to his younger brothers, and now that he's an adult, he is one of my dearest friends. I like him so much.

Then there's my youngest son, Jordan. He is a generous, kind teenager who often surprises me with his sideways sense of humor. Just the other day he walked up to me, placed his hands on my shoulders as if he had something very important to say, and started in with, "Mom, I've decided I don't like clowns." Just as quickly he turned around and started to walk away. When I laughed and asked him why, he looked over his shoulder and said, "Anyone *that* happy is bound to turn on you!" Jordan and I love to spend time playing

Ping-Pong. We are pretty evenly matched, but whenever I pull ahead by several points, he breaks out into this dance. He hops on one foot, then the other, with his arms flailing all over as he returns every ball I send his way. I start laughing at him and I can't stop. He wins every time. He's a great athlete, and one of my favorite pastimes is watching him play football or basketball. I love to spend time with him, and he makes me laugh every day. I really like my Jordan.

Luke is my middle son, and if you've ever heard me speak, you've heard me tell many stories about this one. He is now a gentle giant of a teenager, but he used to be a feisty, strong-willed child who spent more time in the corner than he did anywhere else. He and I laugh together now about those days. He thinks he should receive a share of my speaking fees since he's supplied me with much of my material.

Along with his strong-willed, feisty side, Luke also possessed the most unassuming nature. It's as though it never ever occurred to him to care what others might be thinking about him. One day while dressing for preschool, he asked if *he* could pick out his whole outfit. We headed for the car with Luke wearing his younger brother's shorts (too short, too tight) and a too-large, long-sleeved shirt *covered by* a small, tight T-shirt. Imagine. But that wasn't the worst of it. As he marched out to the car, each footstep made a different sound because he had a dress shoe on one foot and a snowmobile boot on the other.

When he was about five and we were planning his birthday party, Luke listed every person he wanted to invite. One of the names on his list was Bob Ziedler. What's funny about that is Bob was our friend and in his thirties at the time. But Bob always had time for Luke, and Luke wanted him at his party. So Luke's party list consisted of several five-year-olds and one thirty-year-old—and he thought nothing of it.

I'm going to tell you one more story, and trust me, there is a point to all of this. Back when Luke was about eight or nine years old, we signed him up for after-school karate. He was absolutely adorable in his little uniform. I watched him from the side of the gym. The kids were all lined up waiting for personal instruction on proper form from their instructor. Several of the boys toward the end of the line got antsy from waiting, so they took turns running and throwing themselves into a mat that was attached to the wall, falling to the ground, and laughing. Luke was about fifth from the back of the line and enjoyed watching the boys throw themselves against the wall. A couple of them noticed him and asked, "Why don't you try it?" Luke paused, and they said, "C'mon. Ya chicken?" So Luke took in a deep breath, ran hard, and threw himself into the mat with all the strength he had. At that precise moment the instructor looked up and noticed that Luke was out of line. He stood up, yelled at Luke, asked him what he was thinking, and made an example out of him. Luke's cheeks were bright red with embarrassment. The other boys quietly giggled while Luke stood alone.

At that moment I was overcome with affection for my son. I knew he shouldn't have stepped out of line the way he did, but I saw the whole thing. I knew what part was his, and we would talk about that later, but I also knew he felt embarrassed and exposed, and I cared far more about how the whole scenario made him feel about himself than I did his getting out of line. More than anything I wanted him to know how much I loved him.

Comprehending the Incredible Love of God

It's just like that with God—even more so.

If I, being a sinful, selfish human being, have the capacity to cherish my boys in this way and to see the bigger picture in their lives, how much more does a loving God care for us? God loves you. He is holy and powerful. He sees when you've been set up and knows when you've been overlooked. He never looks away, He always hears you, and He listens to what is on your heart. He fully enjoys you, and it pleases His heart so much when you take the leap of faith to believe that someone as wonderful as He would love to be at your party.

Do you know what nourishes the soul? It is knowing (and believing) that we are the object of God's intimate and powerful love. This is at the core of living a healthy, balanced life. If we build our lives on any other hope, we will be disappointed. But if we wake up every single day and remind ourselves that we are unequivocally loved, cherished, and enjoyed, it will affect how we see ourselves, how we think about others, and what we choose to do with our time.

When we understand that our name is written on His hand, that we are someone He sings and rejoices over, and that every time He thinks of us, it is with a pure heart, we are changed from the inside out. He is concerned about our sin, yes. And as we walk with Him, He will help us grow as His children. But most near to His heart is that *we believe* that we are the object of His love. He came to save us, not to condemn us. *We* are His reward.

So how do we come to understand such a profound truth? It's simple—by *knowing* Him. The Bible tells us that knowing the Holy One results in understanding (Proverbs 9:10). How do we come to know Him? We spend time with Him. We wait quietly in His presence. We pray often and allow Him to get a word in at least just as often. We acknowledge His presence all day long. We trust Him on the dark days and praise Him on the brighter days. To grasp His love, we must stay close to Him. He cannot be to us a vending machine, a distant relative, or a sometimes friend. If we reduce Him to such things, He will love us anyway, but we are the ones who lose.

We have an incredible capacity for God because we are His design. He made us for Himself. We live in a world full of distractions and second-bests. And yet nothing will satisfy or fill us like He will. It is only in His presence that our fullness of joy is found (Psalm 16:11 NKJV). It is in His presence that we find our soul's deepest needs nurtured and cared for because no one loves us or knows what we need like He does. Consider again Proverbs 9:10, "Knowledge of the Holy One results in understanding." As we come to know Him more and more, we will understand Scripture more and more. We will believe that He desires to connect with us more and more. We will trust Him more and more.

In his wonderful book *Song of Songs: The Journey of the Bride,* Brian Simmons wrote:

> Knowing how God sees you is the one true healing balm of the wounded heart. Everything else, every program and therapy, is only a "Band-Aid." God's love heals. It casts out fear and brings confidence. His deep affection removes loneliness and rejection from your heart. His overwhelming love overcomes our insecurities and makes us whole again. This must be learned at the beginning of our journey with Christ, or we will stumble all along the way.[1]

Why is it that we live like paupers in our souls when so much has been provided to us? We commit to more than we have time for and then live lives at a harried, frantic pace. We trade our joy for a high level of stress. What belief makes us do that? Financially we often live beyond our means, spending money we've not yet earned. Is this because we don't trust that God is good? And yet with faith, most of us live far *beneath* our means. We have access to riches in the heavenlies. Study the book of Ephesians, and let your spirit be strengthened by knowing all that you possess in Christ.

Could God have possibly given us more than His Son to express His love for us? And yet He not only offered His pure and precious Son as a sacrifice for our sins, He gave us the Holy Spirit to comfort, guide, and direct us during our journey on earth. Because of Jesus' sacrifice, we have fresh mercies awaiting us with each new day. God has even placed it in the hearts of certain people to love us. When people love us, it is a gift from God.

Every morning He paints a new sky and every night He reveals the stars once again. He didn't do any of these things for His health; He did them for ours. It nourishes us to be fully aware of the ways God is working around us every single day.

> Do you want more and more of God's kindness and peace? Then learn to know him better and better. For as you know him better, he will give you, through his great power, everything you need for living a truly good life: he even shares his own glory and his own goodness with us! (2 Peter 1:2-3 TLB).

My husband is more than six feet tall. He weighs about…well, never mind, but he is a large man. I always groan when he thinks we should scratch one another's back because he has twice the acreage to cover. He is a gentle giant and possesses great strength. There have been a few times where I was sitting in bed at night with a cup of tea and a book, thoroughly enjoying myself, only to have my book and tea thrust out of my hands. My sweet husband was just pulling back the covers to get into bed. One minute I was cozy and comfortable, the next minute I was totally uncovered, looking first at my book and spilt tea and then at my surprised husband. He was simply moving in proportion to his size. He is big and strong, and when he whips the covers back without thinking, he causes a minor earthquake.

But on the more important issues in life, my giant of a husband is a gentle saint. When I am hurting, he sits down, looks me in the eyes, and listens to every word I am saying. When I can't reach something, he gets it for me; when something is too heavy, he lifts it for me; and when I am afraid, he stays by my side. So when he accidentally elbows me in the face while trying to put his arm around me, I understand that his movements are large because he is large.

Now think about the strength of God. Mountains melt like wax before Him (Psalm 97:5). At the blast of His breath the bottom of the sea can be seen (2 Samuel 22:16). When you consider the awesome strength of our Almighty God, think about this: Even though God's strength is immeasurable and unmatched, He deals gently with us. He doesn't muscle His way into our lives and beat us into shape. He is patient with our fears and our wounds, and He leads us at a pace He knows we can keep. If the self-restraint of God doesn't speak of His love, I don't know what does.

Comprehending the incredible love of God has so much more to do with "being" than it does "doing." For that reason, I am not going to give the usual "Steps Toward Health" or "Try This" tips in this chapter. I am going to give you time. Take time to reflect on the fact that of all there is to know and see in this vast universe, God has set His affections on *you*. He loves you and wants to renew every part of your life.

Nourish yourself on the following verses:

> For I am the LORD your God, who stirs up the sea,
> causing its waves to roar. My name is the LORD Almighty.
> And I have put my words in your mouth and hidden

you safely within my hand. I set all the stars in space and established the earth. I am the one who says to Israel, "You are mine!" (Isaiah 51:15-16).

Golden splendor comes from the mountain of God. He is clothed in dazzling splendor. We cannot imagine the power of the Almighty, yet he is so just and merciful that he does not oppress us. No wonder people everywhere fear him. People who are truly wise show him reverence (Job 37:22-24).

The LORD is good. When trouble comes, he is a strong refuge. And he knows everyone who trusts in him (Nahum 1:7).

The highest angelic powers stand in awe of God. He is far more awesome than those who surround his throne. O LORD God Almighty! Where is there anyone as mighty as you, LORD? Faithfulness is your very character...Happy are those who hear the joyful call to worship, for they will walk in the light of your presence, LORD...You are their glorious strength. Our power is based on your favor (Psalm 89:7-8,15,17).

Drawing Close to God

Do you want something God has not given you yet? Are you waiting for a certain breakthrough? Precious sister, breakthroughs are nothing for Him. When He makes us wait longer than we want, it is the loving care of a Father exercising restraint until our character is developed enough to handle the blessing. Amid our pleading, begging, and positioning ourselves, He waits. Now that's restraint.

Do you continue to doubt His love for you? His fresh mercies offered to you with each new day allow you to rise up once more and take Him at His word. Though His love cost Him everything, and we are so quick to forget, still, every day He offers us a chance to begin again.

Do you long for more of Him in your life? Do you want to draw closer and closer to Him, that He may conquer every part of your heart? Our spirit is willing, but our flesh is weak. And yet the Father moves on every prayer that asks for more of Him. He moves into the yielded areas in our lives, separating with the skill of a surgeon what is holy and what is not. He hears our passionate cry and broadens the path beneath our feet. His standard is so high and we so often fall short. He could stoop down to crush us, but He doesn't. He stoops down to make us great, and it is His pleasure to do so. What is your response to Him?

Precious Lamb of God,

You are my Beloved and I am Yours. Thank You for giving me grace and mercy I can barely comprehend. You've lavished Yourself upon me, even though I will never fully understand it. Lord, help me to know Your heart. Increase my capacity to know Your love. I want You to fill every low and empty place. I want every anxiety and worry to be replaced with joy and strength. I will not waste one more day living like a pauper when You have called me to be Your heavenly Bride. Change my heart, change my mind, and change the way I live. Help me to embrace the truth that You thoroughly enjoy me, You sing over me, and You love me with a heart that is true. I love You too. Amen.

Balance Application

This may be the most important chapter in the book. If you forget every other piece of advice, do not forget His love for you. Do not let it get away from you. To stay in the center of His will is to maintain your absolute belief in His love. All of life balances on this fact. When you know your loving Father watches over you, you know that storms have their limit and serve their purpose. You notice when something fresh and new springs up in front of you. You hear when He says, "This is the way, walk ye in it" (Isaiah 31:21 KJV). When we lose sight of His love, we lose. A thousand voices and circumstances tell us otherwise, but none can compare to the One who not only told us, He showed us what love is. Beloved sister, He enjoys you. He thinks you are funny and delightful and thoughtful. He wants you set free from your fears and your past so you can be strengthened for your future. Take Him at His word—His highest desire is for you.

Study Time

1. Read Exodus 15:1-12.

2. Read it again, but this time write down every description of the Lord's mightiness and strength mentioned in each verse:

   a. Verse 1:

   b. Verse 2:

   c. Verse 3:

   d. Verse 4:

   e. Verse 5:

   f. Verse 6:

   g. Verse 7:

   h. Verse 8:

   i. Verse 9:

   j. Verse 10:

   k. Verse 11:

   l. Verse 12:

3. Now read verse 13 of the passage above.

4. He displays His strength and reveals His love. In what ways has His love ransomed you? What areas in your life still need rescuing?

5. Look again at verse 13. Where is He leading us?

6. Do you think it is possible to live in that place while tending to your life here on earth?

7. Write out verse 13 in a personalized prayer.

Ten

Let Him Fill You

Jesus answered, "If you knew the generosity of God and who I am, you would be asking me for a drink, and I would give you fresh, living water."

JOHN 4:10 MSG

ONE EVENING AS I SAT IN THE FRONT ROW OF A retreat center with my head bowed, I whispered a prayer, asking God to bless the words I was about to speak. As the host opened the weekend with announcements and my introduction, I recalled the days of fasting and prayer that had helped prepare me for this retreat. The topic was prayer, and I had done my part in the preparation of my notes, my thoughts, and, most importantly, my heart.

I loved this topic because I am passionate about prayer. For many years, prayer supplied the fuel for my fire, the water for my thirst, and the strength for my heart. I longed for these women to experience a new depth in their relationship with Jesus. I wanted them to seek Him in a more intimate way than they ever had before. There was a picture in my mind of how I wanted the weekend to go, and yet it could not happen without the hand of God guiding our time.

Tell them not to leave the well. The whisper came across my heart and made it beat faster. It was almost time for me to go up and speak, and I was caught completely off guard. Again, the still, small voice whispered, *Tell them not to leave the well.* This time I could see a picture in my mind of an old, strong well made from large stones. It was virtually untouched because around it for miles were thousands of makeshift wells...which were really just holes in the ground. I suddenly had an overwhelming sense that many of the women in the crowd had come to this retreat empty, depleted, and thirsty. I sensed that many of them, out of desperation, often turned to counterfeit sources for a quick relief from pain, loneliness, insecurity, and anger. Turning to the quick fix, they missed the greater blessing God had for them.

I found myself with a choice to make. I had one idea about how the weekend was to go, and God had another. His idea, of course, was better because it was living and breathing and, well, He's God. As the host finished my introduction, I stood up and headed for the podium without my notes. I had butterflies in my stomach because these women had paid me to come and speak about prayer. I had no notes in front of me, only a strong sense that God had something so important on His heart for these precious women that He needed His messenger to be vulnerable, dependent, and flexible. It could not be scripted.

For the next few days I found myself utterly dependent on the Holy Spirit's direction for every message I gave. Because I longed for security and something to hold on to, I was tempted at times to rely on the notes I brought with me. And yet by releasing that security, I saw the supernatural unfold before me.

Throughout the weekend I challenged them, "Don't leave the well. Don't be so uncomfortable with your pain that you rush to a quick fix to cover it up. In your loneliness, in your hard times, and in your waiting, stay by the well until the true, pure water comes. He will come for you, He will bring healing and a new direction for your lives." Women responded in droves. Everywhere I looked, I could see women getting right with God. Anger, unforgiveness, insecurities, fears, and destructive habits were brought to the cross; these women dared to admit their thirst before God, which took great courage. As they waited in His presence, He met them. They were nourished by the living water that washed them from their sin and satisfied their thirsty souls. The weekend became an astounding reminder of how fresh things are when they are from the hand of God.

True Nourishment

Remember, we must regularly push beyond what is comfortable if we want to grow. This is especially true in our spiritual lives. If we stay too long in our comfort zones, we get a false sense of security and a distorted picture of how we're really doing. It's only when we step outside of what we are used to that we realize our need, our hunger, and our smallness (which is why most people don't care to venture out). But this is how we grow. It is when we let our guard down, when we admit our need, and when we acknowledge our hunger that God comes rushing in to meet us.

God knows what will bless us and what will destroy us. He commands our obedience because He has our best interest at heart. He did not offer us all that He had only to be listened to once in a while. Nor was the sacrifice of His Son for our sin only to be considered one of the many options for entrance to heaven. He is the way, the truth, and the life (John 14:6). We can either respond to this priceless gift by trusting His love, emptying ourselves before Him, and allowing Him to transform us, or we can deny the power of the cross and miss the whole reason He came.

Attempting to live with one foot in the kingdom and one foot in the trappings of this world seems almost schizophrenic. What God proclaims and what He asks for demands a strong and genuine response; anything less would mean you are not paying attention to what the cross implies. God's words to us may sometimes sound harsh and unbending, but He is speaking about life-and-death issues here. I am very loving and kind to my boys, but you can bet that I am very strong and unbending on the issues of right and wrong. I will never relax my standard just because "everybody else seems to think it's okay." Kevin and I have always told our boys, "It'll never work to use the 'everybody's doing it' thing with us. We'll never bend our standard to fit the ever-changing values in the world."

God knows how easy it is to do what everybody else is doing. He is also aware how much harder it is to do something different. Notice the love and care in the following verses. Also notice that His promises are contingent upon our obedience:

> The Lord will bless everything you do and will fill your storehouses with grain. The Lord your God will bless you in the land he is giving you. If you obey the commands of the Lord your God and walk in his ways, the Lord will establish you as his holy people as he solemnly promised to do (Deuteronomy 28:8-9).

As you read the next passage, slow down and think about the times you trusted in your own wisdom. Notice the benefit of walking in the fear of the Lord, turning your back on evil, and of giving Him the best of what you have. As uncomfortable as it is to receive correction (from people and/or the Word of God), consider it as something that thrusts you outside of your comfort zone and helps you to grow. Notice also the words "fill" and "overflow" in this passage:

> Don't be impressed with your own wisdom. Instead,
> fear the LORD and turn your back on evil. Then you will
> gain renewed health and vitality. Honor the LORD with
> your wealth and with the best part of everything your
> land produces. Then he will fill your barns with grain,
> and your vats will overflow with the finest wine. My
> child, don't ignore it when the LORD disciplines you,
> and don't be discouraged when he corrects you. For
> the LORD corrects those he loves, just as a father cor-
> rects a child in whom he delights (Proverbs 3:7-12).

As you empty yourself out to be filled by the only One who can
satisfy, you will feel vulnerable. The enemy of your soul will tempt
you to be afraid. God knows that. Read the following verses and be
strengthened by His love for you:

> Don't be afraid, for I am with you. Do not be dis-
> mayed, for *I am your God. I will strengthen you. I will
> help you. I will uphold you* with my victorious right
> hand...the joy of the LORD will *fill you to overflowing.
> You will glory in the Holy One of Israel* (Isaiah 41:10,16,
> emphasis added).

He deserves our trust. He is so faithful and strong. That is why
the enemy works tirelessly to keep us from knowing what we possess in the Lord. Speaking of the enemy...he comes to steal what's
been given to you, kill all that's thriving around you, and destroy
your hopes and dreams. Thankfully, God is far more powerful than
the enemy of your soul, and He offers to help you do more than just
survive; He wants you to thrive.

> The thief comes only to steal and kill and destroy; I came that they may have life, and have it abundantly (John 10:10 RSV).

> The thief's purpose is to steal and kill and destroy. My purpose is to give life in all its fullness (John 10:10).

He Has More for You

I am sure you've noticed by now that we are looking at verses that speak of being filled. Even as I write them for you, my own faith is being strengthened. Do you want to be "filled with the fullness of the life and power that comes from God"? Ask God to bring this next verse to life for you:

> May you experience the love of Christ, though it is so great you will never fully understand it. *Then* you will be filled with the fullness of life and power that comes from God (Ephesians 3:19, emphasis added).

In order to grow spiritually, there must be an increase; an increase in hunger, thirst, and knowledge of the One who makes all things grow, so that you can grow into the fullness of all you were created for.

> *You must* crave pure spiritual milk *so that* you can grow into the fullness of your salvation. Cry out for this nourishment as a baby cries for milk, now that you have had a taste of the Lord's kindness (1 Peter 2:2-3, emphasis added).

Ask Him. Ask Him to heal you, fill you, deliver you, and make you whole. If you ask Him, He will do it. His process may be different than what you expect, but there's no mistaking freedom. When you're free and full, you won't wonder about it; *you'll know*. Beloved sister, let Him fill every dark and dreary place, every low and lonely place, every budding hope and dream. Ask Him to work wonders in your life. He will.

Read God's invitation to you. Give Him your full attention. I promise you, there's not a better offer out there.

> Hey there! All who are thirsty, come to the water! Are you penniless? Come anyway—buy and eat! Come, buy your drinks, buy wine and milk. Buy without money—everything's free! Why do you spend your money on junk food, your hard-earned cash on cotton candy? Listen to me, listen well: Eat only the best, fill yourself with only the finest. Pay attention, come close now, listen carefully to my life-giving, life-nourishing words. I'm making a lasting covenant commitment with you, the same that I made with David: sure, solid, enduring love…Seek God while he's here to be found, pray to him while he's close at hand. Let the wicked abandon their way of life and the evil their way of thinking. Let them come back to God, who is merciful, come back to our God, who is lavish with forgiveness (Isaiah 55:1-3,6-7 MSG).

As we move into the topic of how we nourish our souls, be encouraged to know that no matter where you are with God, whether you've wandered away, stayed close, or never officially met Him, He has more for you. Whatever aspects of His character you have discovered, there are countless other treasures yet to be uncovered in your relationship with Him. Remember, the Bible tells us that it is in *His* presence where our *fullness* of joy is found (Psalm 16:11 NKJV). *Nothing* satisfies like He does. Every empty place, every hunger, and every hope will find its fullness in the abounding, immeasurable presence of God.

We have a snack cupboard in our home where we keep raisins, trail mix, snack bars, popcorn, etc. When you open that cupboard, you see a big sign that says, "No Snacks on an Empty Stomach!" My three big teenage boys could easily polish off everything in that cupboard in a matter of minutes. In fact, they've done it before. Then, when dinnertime rolled around, they had no room for the good stuff. Their bellies were full, but their bodies remained unnourished.

Ecclesiastes 6:7 says, "We work to feed our appetites; meanwhile our souls go hungry" (MSG). When we fill ourselves up on the things of the world, we have a sense of "fullness" while our spiritual lives go unnourished. Our quick fix society allows us access to things so we never have to fully experience certain levels of hunger, pain, desire, or loneliness. We eat, we shop, we drink, we watch, and we medicate… and then we miss out on the deeper life. Obviously, this is not to say that eating food, buying certain items, watching certain movies, or taking certain medicines is bad. It's only bad when those things are used to fill a place that was meant for God.

When we come to the place where we can honestly admit and face our need, He will honestly meet us there. Honesty sounds something like this: "The truth is, it's especially in a large crowd that I feel alone. That's why I get loud and draw all kinds of attention to myself " or "The truth is, I am still very angry, and I don't know how not to be, so I drink or I eat" or "The truth is, I cannot let go of my past, so I am constantly striving to achieve and prove my worth" or

"The truth is, I always feel 'less than,' so I go shopping and buy things that are 'better than.'"

When we quit filling ourselves up on the junk food of this world and allow ourselves to feel the emptiness, the hunger, and the pain in our souls—and then ask God to do something about it—He will meet us, fill us, and more than satisfy our deepest needs.

Father in heaven,

Thank You for loving me. You are long-suffering, patient, and kind. Forgive me for grabbing quick fixes rather than waiting for the best of what You have for me. Lord God, increase my hunger and thirst for You. Help me desire the things that nourish my soul. Grant me the ability to see the bigger picture and to know when I am cutting corners for convenience, which causes me to miss the greater blessing. Give me an eternal perspective so that I might choose life and nourishment every single day. In Your precious name, I pray. Amen.

Steps Toward Health

* I will pause, pray, and ask God to search my heart. I will ask Him to show me what I use to medicate my pain, discomfort, boredom, etc.

* I will lay this thing down for a time (a partial fast) for the purpose of seeking a deeper walk with the Lord.

* I will share this with a godly friend for the sake of accountability.

* I will remember every day as I wrestle with the temptations

and distractions of life that I am someone God thoroughly enjoys.

* I will continue to pursue a more simple life.

TRY THIS

* *Pause regularly and pray.* "Nourish my soul, Lord. Make me whole. May my life reflect more of You and less of me. Create in me a heart to do Your will, to see things from Your perspective, and to serve You above all. Amen."

* *Pursue and protect your devotional times.* Spend regular time with God. Look forward with expectation to increased amounts of time with Him.

* *Every morning proclaim, "I'm alive in Christ!"* Say this out loud and let these words trump every lesser message that comes your way. Look for Him throughout the day. He provides nourishment in many creative ways. Allow Him to nourish you.

* *Pray before you read the Word of God.* Ask for an increased capacity to understand the hidden truths in the Word of God. Ask the Lord to use the Word to speak directly into your life. This will radically change your perspective and priorities.

* *Meet Him in a different place.* Don't allow your devotional life to become rote or commonplace. Keep your love affair alive. Sometimes I lie face down on the floor and pray, "Oh, Father, if I could get any lower I would; You are so holy; have mercy on this soul of mine." Other times I recline in His presence and just rest in Him. I approach Him as an intimate love and friend. Often I will sit in total silence for extended periods of time. He is my Counselor, and when I spend more time listening than talking, my soul is nourished. Sometimes when

I'm all alone in my house, I twirl and dance to a beautiful song. I celebrate all He has provided, and it makes me want to dance.

* *Place Scripture where you spend a lot of time.* Find a verse that ministers to your heart. Look often at the Scripture, think about it, look out the window, and breathe a prayer to God.

* *Find an accountability partner.* Choose someone you know is serious about following the Lord. Dare to ask the hard questions of one another like, "More important than how you are feeling, how are you *thinking* lately?" or "How is your devotional life?" or "Are your relationships clean?" Meet regularly. Begin and end your meetings with prayer. This will help keep you on track.

* *Cherish the quiet.* When you come upon a quiet moment, don't fill it with noise. Don't call a friend every time. Don't turn on the TV. Every once in a while, allow those sacred times to become Sabbath moments. Acknowledge Him in the quiet. Whether you feel Him or not, He will nourish you.

* *Lie down and look up.* Every once in a while, put some praise music on, lie down, and picture yourself in the presence of God. Just rest there. I promise it will do something for you.

Balance Application

God will fill us when we're not filling ourselves with something else. To maintain a life of balance, we must stay close to and be nourished by our Source of life. We may last a little while on the world's junk food, but it will ultimately fail us. Every day we deposit things into our lives. We often don't see the results of those deposits right away. At first they create "invisible changes." Eventually, our inward choices catch up with our outward lives. We have the choice each day to either "just get by" or to boldly invest in something much bigger than ourselves. God is everywhere and doing many things, but the significance is lost on us because we are too busy and too distracted. There are spiritual parallels and connections in almost anything we do: from gardening to baking, from loving our children to loving our spouse. God's truths and His lessons are woven into the fabric of life. God is speaking and pouring Himself out to a waiting and watching world. The problem is, the majority are neither waiting nor watching. Oh, may we feast on the best of what God has for us. There's a world out there in need of the fresh life to which we have access.

Study Time

1. Read Mark 8:1-8. In a few sentences, summarize what happened here. For instance, describe Jesus' heart for the people, describe the need, describe the process of meeting the need, and describe the outcome.

2. Think about that for a moment. People investing their

time, risking hunger just to have more of Jesus. Seven loaves, four thousand plus people. The multitudes ate until they were *full*. More than enough was left over. How big is our God?

3. Read Mark 8:11. Recall a time in your own life where someone came to you with the intent to accuse and argue with you. How did that feel? Imagine Jesus. He had just ministered to thousands of people with great care and compassion. He immediately hops in the boat to go to the next place and is confronted by prideful, accusatory religious leaders. Describe how you think He felt.

4. Read Mark 8:12. What was Jesus' response to their demands? Why do you think He responded this way? Explain.

5. Read Mark 8:13-14. The disciples forgot their food for the day. Just a note here: Even when we forget, God is still enough.

6. Now read Mark 8:15. Recall again that time when you were verbally "assaulted" by someone. As I mentioned earlier in the book, it can take your nervous system up to two days to settle down from an intense confrontation. Jesus loves His disciples and is concerned that as their ministry grows, that they not become prideful, demanding, and arrogant. With that in mind, read verse 15 again.

7. Read Mark 8:16. Contrast the disciples' concerns and perspective with that of Jesus'.

8. Read Mark 8:17-21. Hear the passion in Jesus' voice. He

is exasperated that after they witnessed such an incredible miracle, their eyes so quickly went back to their appetite and immediate need. Think about that in terms of your own life. (Take your time. This deserves some thought.) We must remember that without faith, it is *impossible* to please Him (see Hebrews 11:6).

9. It's as if Jesus is saying, "Concern yourselves not with provision; I own it all. Concern yourselves with the poison of pride. Don't strive to satisfy your appetite, be earnest in guarding your heart." We often mix up our job and God's job. In spite of the good things God has done for you, are there areas in your life where you worry more than trust? Write them down. Write a prayer asking for forgiveness and asking God for more faith.

10. Pause and pray that you would be *filled* with more of God and that your perspective would reflect a heart of faith.

Eleven

A Healthy Spiritual Diet

*An intelligent person is always eager to take
in more truth; fools feed on fast-food fads
and fancies.*

PROVERBS 15:14 MSG

EVERY TIME I PREPARE FOR A SPEAKING ENGAGEMENT, I enter a
time of fasting. I fast from certain foods or meals, I fast from media,
and I even sometimes fast from the telephone. I use that extra time
for prayer, study of the Word, and extended periods of silence in
God's presence. This allows me time to focus and prepare my heart,
and most of all, to hear from God. It's especially during my times of
silence that I get the clearest sense of what I am supposed to say at
the upcoming engagement.

When my events are over, I come home to be greeted by my boys
and my husband. After I drop my bags in the entryway, we all gather
in the living room and I share how God moved in the hearts of the
women. I often choke up when I describe some of the significant ways
women were ministered to. We sometimes pray together to thank the
Lord for what He's done and what He will continue to do. After this
sweet time with my family, I unpack my bags and then usually

snuggle up with a favorite novel, a bowl of popcorn, and the remote control (so I can see what's going on in the news). When my kids were younger, I didn't have this luxury. I am thankful for and love this time of rest and replenishment.

Well, after one particular event, God moved in such a profound way that it left me speechless. In fact, I heard from a woman who said it took her three days to find the words to share how God touched her during this time. Another woman wrote to me and said that she walked into the session with a severe sinus infection and she walked out without one. I was not speaking on the subject of healing; I was talking about prayer. But the presence of God was so strong in that sanctuary, I could have said nothing and women would have experienced God in a profound way.

I came home unable to even consider indulging in my usual treats. There was nothing sinful or excessive about my little treats, but at that moment they didn't sound good to me. I was exhausted, but more than that, I was hungry; not physically hungry, but *starving* for more of what I experienced at that event. Clearly, I tasted something that was far beyond me.

I felt compelled to continue my fast for the sake of gaining a deeper understanding of what God had just done. I crawled into bed and pulled the covers up around me. I prayed myself to sleep with, "Lord, I want more of You. Show me more of You."

Curled up in a little ball, whispering my prayer to the Lord, I began to doze off and dream. In my dream I saw a deep blue, purplish sky with clouds rumbling and moving. Lightning was shooting through the darkness. This display of God's power hovered just overhead. Below, people walked along chatting, completely unaware of the powerful sight just above them. Occasionally a mother would stop, reach up, grab a handful of the "power," put it on her children, and then go about her business. Some never looked up; they just walked along, totally caught up in their earthly affairs. Others looked up and took hold of the power only in times of crisis. But every once in a while, you would see someone who took hold of every ounce she could grab to place it on her kids, her marriage, and her own heart. It was as though she found the secret to a powerful life and was going to lay hold of everything made available to her. She would not be distracted by the things around her; she had found the Source of power.

As I woke up and pondered this unusual dream, the Lord spoke to my heart and said, *Most of my children only scratch the surface of what I have made available to them. If they took hold of everything they had access to, they would change the world.* I was so impacted by my speaking event and the dream that followed that I have never stopped praying, "Lord God, help me to lay hold of all You've laid hold of for me. I want to fulfill every last thing You created me for!"

Try to imagine the power God has made available to us. Imagine if we traded our addictions and bad habits for soul nourishment that would heal us, give us a holy confidence, and a strong sense of purpose. What if, instead of living lives where we constantly struggle with overindulgence, always feeding our appetites and comforts, we instead looked to God to meet needs only He was meant to fulfill? Wouldn't it be something to become "flow through accounts" where we continually accessed all that God wants to give *to* us and *through* us? What if we gained such freedom from the snares of this world that our lives were freed up to live powerfully, to be walking, breathing representatives of the Most High God? Can you imagine how we would change the world? Read the following passages and ask God to help you grasp all that's available to you:

> I pray that you will begin to understand *the incredible
> greatness of his power for us who believe him. This is the*

same mighty power that raised Christ from the dead and seated him in the place of honor at God's right hand in the heavenly realms (Ephesians 1:19-20, emphasis added).

I pray that from his glorious, unlimited resources he will give you mighty inner strength through his Holy Spirit... Now glory be to God! By his mighty power at work within us, *he is able to accomplish infinitely more than we would ever dare to ask or hope* (Ephesians 3:16,20, emphasis added).

What does this have to do with having a healthy spiritual diet? Everything. Most people eat healthy food because it is good for them. Over time they acquire a taste for it and actually prefer it over junk food. But to start with, there is usually a certain understanding that motivates people to eat healthy. They want to carry around less weight, they want to feel better, they want more energy, they want to reduce their chance of disease, and they want to maintain a youthful appearance. Once a person begins to reap the benefits of a healthy diet, they tend to prefer the discipline over the path of least resistance.

As we look at various ways to nourish your soul, remember the lever principle. Every one of us has a certain level of "input" in our lives, both physically and spiritually. What changes from season to season is the degree that we take in. So there will be seasons in which you are able to take in more, and there will be seasons in which you are forced to live on less. As long as the other levers (output and rest) also adjust at the same time, you will be able to maintain a certain sense of balance wherever life finds you.

That said, we must also remember that God's supply is never

short. Whether we are in a season raising our little ones, have school-age kids, or are at the bedside of a loved one who is ill, God *will* supply *all* our needs. Our part is to seize every moment we can throughout our day to acknowledge God, ask for His help and direction, and then listen for His voice. One of my favorite verses is Psalm 116:9, "I walk in the LORD's presence as I live here on earth!" If we approach every day with the mind-set that God is with us and longs for us to draw on His strength, we will find strength for the task, wisdom for direction, and love that fills every gap. Precious sister, draw near to Him. He is waiting to give you more.

Nourishment for My Spiritual Body

How wonderful it is to have a heavenly Father who is endless in His love for us and boundless in His supply on our behalf. When we plumb the depths of the power of God in our lives, nothing else compares. His mercies are new every morning and His faithfulness is beyond our comprehension (Lamentations 3:22-23 NKJV). We have access to all of God's riches, which leaves us without reason for living a stale and stagnant life. Jesus said to His disciples, "I have food you don't know about" (John 4:32), and again He said, "My nourishment comes from doing the will of God, who sent me, and from finishing his work" (John 4:34).

Since Jesus is our Source, it is important to remember what our spiritual food is for:

Spiritual food is for drowning our sorrows. "Surely He took up our infirmities and carried our sorrows" (Isaiah 53:4 NIV) As we feed on the Word of God and spend time in His presence, He will heal us, deliver us, and get us back on our feet again. You may be going through grief or a time of loss, and the Word of God is full of verses that will identify with your pain and comfort you in your sorrow. The

Bible is also filled with hope, and as you think on the verses that mean something to you, you will find your soul restored.

Spiritual food is an outlet for our anger. "But you, O LORD, are a compassionate and gracious God, slow to anger, abounding in love and faithfulness" (Psalm 86:15 NIV). People will hurt and betray you. They will treat you unkindly and if you are human, this will make you mad. But when you bring your anger to the Lord, when you humble yourself before Him and confess your own sin, He becomes your greatest defender. When you submit yourself to Him, He will help you to let go of the anger and gain victory over your situation.

Spiritual food is an outlet for boredom. "LORD, you have brought light to my life; my God, you light up my darkness" (Psalm 18:28). Often when we are bored it is because we have lost our sense of gratitude and wonder. The Bible says that God inhabits the praises of His people (Psalm 22:3 KJV). Try this once. Take a few moments and start thanking the Lord for everything you can think of...*Thank You, Lord, for running water and for a roof over my head. Thank You, Lord, for the laughter of my children. Thank you, Lord, for my eyesight...*If you take a moment to enter the presence of the Living God, your perspective will change and your soul will be nourished beyond belief.

Spiritual food is not only meant to fuel us. It is for our enjoyment too. "The LORD is my shepherd; I have everything I need. He lets me rest in green meadows; he leads me beside peaceful streams. He renews my strength. He guides me along right paths, bringing honor to his name" (Psalm 23:1-3). Just as we acquire a taste for certain foods, we acquire a hunger for the presence of the Lord as we spend more and more time with Him. If you struggle with even having a desire to nourish yourself spiritually, start there. Be honest and pray, "Lord, I have no desire to draw near. Please make me hunger for

Your Word and Your Presence. Help me know You are all I need. Amen."

Spiritual Food Laws to Live By

Keep it colorful. Do not overload on only one choice of nourishment (for example, one speaker, one author, one musician). Jesus has equipped a multitude of His children for the building up of His kingdom. When you feast on the fruit of only one of His servants, you run the risk of becoming narrow in your thinking and acceptance of how things should be communicated. God speaks in many ways, even through donkeys (see Numbers 22:21-33), and it is His great pleasure to do so. Be open to all He is saying and doing around you. Listen to your children; He often speaks through them. When you humble yourself and acquire a taste for the different reflections of Christ's character, you will be more well-rounded.

A secret isn't a secret. Walk in the light where there is fellowship, freedom, and peace. Be real about your struggles. If you can't go to church to get free, where can you? Things feel so much bigger when they are kept hidden. The truth is that you are not alone, you are not the first to struggle in this area, and nothing is worth hiding when it keeps us from freedom. The enemy of your soul will try to convince you that keeping your struggles in the dark will keep you from being exposed, but *he* doesn't want to be exposed for the liar he is. Jesus died for your sins. When you bring your struggles into the light, you can see them for what they are. When you bring them to the cross, you can get set free. "When I refused to confess my sin, I was weak and miserable, and I groaned all day long" (Psalm 32:3). "Yes, what joy for those whose record the LORD has cleared of sin, whose lives are lived in complete honesty!" (Psalm 32:2). For further study, see 1 John 1:7-9.

Look past it. One day I was preoccupied about a number of things. I caught myself staring out the window as I mulled my worries over in my mind. Well, I wasn't actually staring out the window; I was staring *at* the window. There was this dirty spot on the window that caught my gaze. My eyes landed on that spot while my mind ran wild with things I had no control over. Out of the corner of my eye I saw movement. I snapped out of my daydream to see a jogger running by. Then I looked up and saw the trees blowing in the breeze. A red cardinal landed on a nearby branch. It was a lovely day and a perfect lesson. How often do we fix our minds and our focus on our worries and miss the bigger picture? Yes, we need to acknowledge our problems, but we should not fixate on them. Scripture tells us to keep our eyes on Jesus (Hebrews 12:2). Every day, more often than not, acknowledge your need, bring it to God, and then look past your circumstances to the handiwork of God. Remind yourself that if He can create a world in six days, He can solve your problems without much effort.

Remember the metabolic rule. If we go too long without "eating," our spiritual metabolism will slow down and we will begin to lose our taste for the things of God. Going too long without nourishing our souls will cause a decline in our spiritual energy. Once we have surrendered to Christ, we are a new creation. But if we pay little attention to nourishing our souls, we affect our fellowship with Him. If our fellowship with Jesus is weak, *we* will be weak and will have little strength to stand when the storms hit. Take moments throughout the day to notice the sky and breathe a prayer. Buy a flip calendar with Scripture verses and quotations and look at it regularly throughout the day. Carry a small book in your purse—one that challenges your spiritual walk—and open it up when you are in the waiting room, the grocery line, etc. Feed your soul regularly throughout the day.

Do "eat" at night. Though it is best not to eat food at night, it is wonderful to end your day with a little soul nourishment. Keep a devotional by your bedside and close the day with thoughts of grace to cover your mistakes, faith that God will protect everything you love, and hope for a fruitful day tomorrow. The Bible says that it is good to praise the Lord, to proclaim His love in the morning, and His faithfulness at night (Psalm 92:2).

Practice partial fasts. I covered this in the first section, but I want to address it again on a slightly deeper level. Whenever you deprive yourself of something that you're selfish about having, it will be difficult at first. Just as fasting from food starts a detoxification process that, among other things, is revealed on the tongue, fasting from things we have an unhealthy attachment to also brings things to the surface of the tongue. You may become edgy, you may say things you don't mean, and you may even become angry. As soon as some people encounter these unpleasant "symptoms," they return to their *thing* and the symptoms go away. The fact that there *is* a response is all the more reason to press through and get victory over the thing that has a hold on you.

Listen. Really listen. When you approach each day with your ears wide open, expecting God to speak to you, you will be nourished beyond your expectations. Next time you hear a worship song on the radio, focus your attention on the words and ponder how they apply to you. Listen to your children. Next time they have something to say to you, stop what you are doing, get low, and look them right in the eye. Take in all of their features and delight in the way God designed them. Hear their words and be blessed by their presence in your life. When a friend compliments you, let it in. Allow yourself to be nourished by her words. Next time you're in church, listen closely to the sermon. Ask the Lord to show you what your response should be to the message you've just heard. Listen to the birds sing. Listen to laughter. Be selective about what you listen to.

Guard your heart. Keep your heart a sacred place—don't let weeds of bitterness and discontentment sprout up. This requires an intentional pursuit of purity. As soon as you notice yourself picking up an offense against someone or something, get down on your knees and relinquish your rights to the Lord. God will at times allow very hurtful and unjust things to happen to us. What I have learned through many of these trials was that God was at work, purifying my heart, renewing my mind, and strengthening my resolve to love. This is no small task. Purity, humility, and love are not flowery, gooey emotions. They are traits wrought through the thickest of battles and the fiercest of fights. No one just happens upon a heart that is free of malice and hardness. Love and guard your heart and keep it a sweet and fresh place.

Take responsibility for your spiritual health. It is not your pastor's job or your husband's job or your friend's job to make sure you stay on track. Granted, the Lord wants us to surround ourselves with people who can be of benefit to our spiritual health, but you are the one who will decide what attitudes you will embrace, what thoughts you will entertain, and where you will spend your time. You will stand before God and give account for the return He receives on His investment in you. Ask the Lord to reveal to you where you are weak. This is good for you to know because you can bet that the enemy of your soul knows not only your weaknesses, he knows how you can be tempted. This is why, as uncomfortable as it is, we must honestly face our spiritual deficiencies so that our walls can be fortified and we can stand strong when the elements rage.[1] Don't look for excuses for your weakness. Look instead for ways to be strengthened.

Use your strength. When you feel strong in the Lord, use that strength to take extra ground. In other words, pray longer, serve lovingly, and listen more. If God has given you a special time of favor, it isn't just for your health. It is because He has something more for you to do and He trusts you to do it. If you feel weak and fragile, hang on to this verse: "A bruised reed he will not break, and a dimly burning wick he will not quench; he will faithfully bring forth justice" (Isaiah 42:3 RSV). Picture Him cupping His hands around you as the elements rage. Imagine Him protecting you while the wind blows. He will breathe new life and strength into you. Take Him at His word. When you are weak, hang on. When you are strong, take extra ground.

Join a Bible study. There are many wonderful Bible studies. Powerful things happen when women come together for the purpose of fellowship and spiritual growth. Whether you believe it or not, you have much to offer other women and they have much to offer you. We really need each other. You might be surprised to find when you show up on those days when it would have been easier to stay at home, that God will especially use you, speak to you, or bless you in some special way.

Carve out your quiet time. As I mentioned earlier, years ago when my sons were little boys, I was fighting a terrible disease at the same time. My little ones were close in age and combining that with my sickness, life was anything but settled and peaceful. I came into my marriage accustomed to regular quiet times, and yet my life drastically changed almost overnight. I went to the Lord *regularly* and passionately appealed to Him, "You are capable of moving heaven and earth for Your children. I want time with You. You want time with me. Your Word promises that when I ask for something in accordance with Your will, I can be sure that I'll receive it. I will spend my pitiful ten minutes doing devotions since that's all the quiet time available for me right now. I will show up for my quiet times and consider them a 'tithe of the time.' I trust that as I give

You my few minutes, You'll see me as You did the boy on the hill-side who gave You his lunch. You multiplied his gift beyond belief! I trust You to multiply my devotional time beyond belief. I want to walk closely with You—You want this for me too. I will watch and see what You will do."

A miraculous thing happened; the boys began playing together for longer periods of time without incident. Now, I will confess, I did sort of tell them that unless they were hemorrhaging they needed to play nicely until I was done praying, but they got used to the priority of my prayer time. Over time, with three little, active boys, the Lord provided ample amounts of study and prayer time. He became my strength through the darkest of valleys. Give Him what little time you have. Ask Him to give you more, and expect that He will. He loves prayers like that because He loves to spend time with you.

A.W. Tozer wrote this regarding your time with the Lord:

> Retire from the world each day to some private spot, even if it be only the bedroom (for a while I retreated to the furnace room for want of a better place). Stay in the secret place till the surrounding noises begin to fade out of your heart and a sense of God's presence envelops you. Deliberately tune out the unpleasant sounds and come out of your closet determined not to hear them. Listen for the inward voice till you learn to recognize it. Stop trying to compete with others. Give yourself to God and then be what and who you are without regard to what others think. Reduce your interests to a few. Don't try to know what will be of no service to you...Pray for a single eye. Read less, but read more of what is important to your inner life.

Never let your mind remain scattered for very long. Call home your roving thoughts. Gaze on Christ with the eyes of your soul. Practice spiritual concentration.[2]

God in heaven,

I long to have more of You. Take me to that higher place, Lord. Keep me from swallowing the world's lies when You've prepared for me a feast of healing truths. Help me to take You at Your word. Increase my capacity to know You. Increase my desire to spend time in Your presence. More than anything, help me grasp Your love for me, for that will affect everything I think and do. I hunger for You, Lord. Make me hunger more. Amen.

Steps Toward Health

- I will take an honest look at my spiritual diet. I will consider it a priority to take the steps needed to nourish myself spiritually.

- I will not feel guilty or consider it a waste of time to sit down to pray or to just be quiet before the Lord. I will think of these times as an investment and know that God will bring a great return in my life and the lives around me as a result.

- I will ask God which of the Spiritual Food Laws I need to apply in my life.

- I will refuse to look at this information as yet another impossible list of things I must accomplish; rather, I will pick and choose those things that will help me be spiritually healthy.

- I will ask God to increase my hunger for Him.

TRY THIS

* Purchase Mary Tileston's book *Joy & Strength*. This inexpensive little devotional is packed with words from giants of the faith. If you want a colorful spiritual diet, nourish yourself on the wisdom of those who have gone before us.

* Rent the movie *The Hiding Place*. Allow this film to speak to you on many levels. Be thankful for the freedom and provisions you enjoy. Be inspired by the tenacity of this family's faith. Notice how Corrie and her sister adjust to their wretched circumstances. They found a place of fruitfulness in the darkness of a prison camp. Amid their struggle, they were nourished by God's Word, and they gave it away.

* Dare to ask God this question: Lord, what do I have in my hand that You want, so that I can take hold of more of You?

* Spend less time indulging yourself this week and more time nourishing yourself.

* Buy a notebook or a journal and begin to record the things God is speaking to you (this will nourish you now *and* later when you look back on it).

* Make it your practice to keep your ears and eyes wide open all day long. Be aware of all that God is doing around you. Obey Him when He tells you to do something.

Balance Application

The heavens are bursting with blessing, provision, and promise. God waits for us and longs to bless us. Every time we look up and call on Him to influence our lives, He will. Every time we go without something for the purpose of seeking Him more, we will receive far more than we gave up. When we embrace every sacred moment that comes our way as a chance to love God more, listen to His voice, and do what He says, our life becomes a living, breathing example of Christ's continued work on earth. To be nourished by the Most High God is our greatest privilege. It's what gives us the strength to do things that are far beyond us.

Study Time

1. Read Hebrews 12:1.

2. What are the weights in your life that slow you down?

3. What things do you get tangled up in?

4. If Jesus was sitting right next to you, what do you think He would tell you about these things? What will you do about them?

5. Read Luke 12:22-30. Read it again.

6. Share or write how this passage applies to you.

7. Look at Luke 12:31.

8. What is the promise? What's the contingency?

9. Are there changes you need to make in your life so you

can better nourish yourself (so you'll be better strengthened for kingdom work)?

10. Write down a prayer asking God to help you do what
He is calling you to do.

Twelve
A Healthy Thought Life

Fix your thoughts on what is true and honorable and right. Think about things that are pure and lovely and admirable. Think about things that are excellent and worthy of praise.

PHILIPPIANS 4:8

W HEN I WAS YOUNG, I WAS VIOLATED BY SEVERAL teenage boys in our neighborhood. One day I was a naive, innocent girl; the next day I was fearful, anxious, and all too aware of my "nakedness." For the rest of my teen years and most of my young adult life, I tried to crawl out of my black hole of insecurity. I leaned heavily upon my physical ability in the hope that my achievements would balance the scales in my mind. I didn't want the "lost cause" side to win. Unfortunately, covering lies with achievements do not turn lies into truths.

Though I was a passionate Christian, I lacked real freedom and peace. Though I consistently spent time with the Lord, read the Bible, and memorized Scripture, I couldn't hang on to the joy God had promised me. One day while watching an old cartoon with my kids, I got a very clear picture of myself. (It was quite a few years ago so I can't remember the cartoon. I think it was Bugs Bunny.) One of the characters was hit with several arrows. He pulled out the arrows and went about his day. Later on he drank a glass of milk, and guess what happened? *He leaked!* That was me! I was depositing wonderful truths and wisdom into my life, but much of it leaked out. An inconsistent thought life kept me from "keeping" all God was making available to me. First John 2:24 says, "See that what you have heard from the beginning remains in you" (NIV).

Guard Your Thought Life

Sometimes I embraced the truth. Other times I mulled over my mistakes. I found that if I spent too much time on the mistakes, the devil tacked onto my train of thought a caboose filled with condemnation, accusation, and insecurity.

Did you know that insecurity is just another form of selfishness? When our thoughts are wrapped up in all that is wrong with us or all that we lack, we miss what's beautiful around us and in us. When we are insecure (or prideful, for that matter), we make decisions with "me" in mind.

Our youngest son, Jordan, is now a teenager. When he was young he was terribly shy, sweet, and somewhat insecure. My husband and I prayed for him and constantly told him, "Jordan, you are so important to God and to us. If you are shy in the sense that you have less to say, that's okay. But if you are timid because you are afraid of what people think of you, that's not okay. You have the God of the universe living in your soul, and He commands you not to fear the opinions of others. If you walk in the fear of the Lord, meaning, that you respect Him enough to do what He says, you need fear nothing else. God has put too much into you. Don't shrink back because of what others might think." Those words sunk in over time, and he is now a totally transformed young man. The strengths he possesses were once his weaknesses. Jordan is strong, confident, and funny. He absolutely does not care what people think of him, and yet he remains very kind and considerate of others. What power there is in a life that's free of self.

The Bible tells us that the pure in heart will see God. When our hearts and minds are pure, we are more able to see what God is doing in our own lives and the lives of others. If our thoughts are marred by insecurity, anger, or self-awareness, we miss much of what God is doing and our choices will drive us further and further away from what will truly fill us.

In her wonderful book, *Something More,* Catherine Marshall wrote about a term that was often used during World War II. The term "beachhead" described a battle that usually took place on the shore. Whoever won the beach often won the bigger battle. Catherine Marshall compares this to our thought life. She writes,

> Just so—my life, my body, my affairs are as an island empire that the unholy spirit hopes to win en route to his ultimate objective of my eternal soul. To do that, he too must first gain a beachhead in my life. With that toehold, then he can take his time about gaining control of the rest of me and my affairs—yard by yard, decision by decision.[1]

Look again at the Scripture at the beginning of this chapter and you will find God's standard for a healthy thought life. In that Scripture are eight gatekeepers for guarding your mind. When we intentionally set a watch on our thoughts and refuse entrance to any thought that is beneath God's standard for us, we will literally be transformed. In our pursuit of a higher calling and a healthier life, here lies a nugget of truth we must never let go of: When we don't allow our thoughts to run wild, they will run deeper.

Eight Ways to Keep Your Thought Life Safe

Let's take a look at eight gatekeepers that will guard our freedom and protect our peace. Philippians 4:8 says to "fix your thoughts." Stop there. Amid the whirlwind of life, how does one "fix their thoughts" on *anything?* The best example I can think of is in this little story. I once heard a story about a man who took his young son on a fishing trip. They were in the middle of nowhere when the son desperately needed a bathroom, and the woods wouldn't suffice, if you know what I mean. The only available place was a dive of a bar. It looked pretty run-down and was the last place you would want to take your child.

But in they went, father and son, into the smoky, dingy bar. Once they got into the bathroom, the father noticed there were no doors on the stalls. And even worse than that, there were foul words written all over the walls of the stalls. The boy sat down on the stool and the father knelt right in front of his son. He placed his strong hands on his son's face, got close to him, and said, "Just keep looking at me, son. Just keep looking at me." The boy replied, "Okay, Daddy."

That's what "fixing your eyes" looks like. No matter what foul messages or less than pleasant circumstances surround you, place your precious face in the hands of your Savior and listen to Him. Below are eight ways you can help your thought life be healthy.

Gatekeeper 1—Fix your thoughts on what is true. "As for God, his way is perfect. All the LORD's promises prove true. He is a shield for all who look to him for protection" (Psalm 18:30). "For the word of the LORD holds true, and everything he does is worthy of our trust"

(Psalm 33:4). There is a big difference between something that *feels* true and something that *is* true. Things that *feel* true often have to do with our value, our situation, or how others see us. We *must* build our thought lives on something far more stable than circumstance. What doesn't change is God's love for you. He is *for* you, not against you. What's also wonderfully true is that every seemingly hopeless situation is a perfect opportunity for God to show you His glory. What's true is that He loves "impossible" situations, because with God all things are possible (see Matthew 19:26). A healthy thought life focuses on the truth.

Gatekeeper 2—Fix your thoughts on what is honorable. "Never pay back evil for evil to anyone. Do things in such a way that everyone can see you are honorable" (Romans 12:17). "Be careful how you live among your unbelieving neighbors. Even if they accuse you of doing wrong, they will see your honorable behavior, and they will believe and give honor to God when he comes to judge the world" (1 Peter 2:12). I once spent a week praying about this gatekeeper. I asked God to show me what it means to have an honorable thought life. Wow, did He show me! Throughout my week, people pulled out in front of me on the road, snapped at me on the phone, and one (not naming names) threw all of his clothes on the floor just two feet shy of the laundry basket. I asked him, "You can estimate the cost of multi-million dollar buildings down to the last screw, but you repeatedly miss the laundry basket by two feet?" Well, that wasn't such an honorable thought, and worse yet, I spoke it while I was thinking it! (We'll address the short connection between the mind and the mouth in a few chapters.) My point is that I was provided countless opportunities to forgive, excuse, pray for, and bless others. It's much more fun to bless a friend with a bouquet of flowers than it is to bless a rude stranger with your smiles, your time, and your prayers. But this is where our walk of faith matters most. This is where we look at and treat people with God's heart in mind. Give some thought to this attribute. Imagine if the world could hear your thoughts all day, every day. A healthy thought life is full of honorable thoughts.

Gatekeeper 3—Fix your thoughts on what is right. "God is my shield, saving those whose hearts are true and right" (Psalm 7:10). "Who may worship in your sanctuary, Lord? Who may enter your presence on your holy hill? Those who lead blameless lives and do what is right, speaking the truth from sincere hearts" (Psalm 15:1-2). We are invited to a deeper place with God, but with the invitation comes a charge to do what is right. Notice that the call is not to fix your thoughts on *your rights,* but rather on what is right before God. It's logical to dislike a selfish neighbor, but as God's child it is *right* to be kind to them and pray for them. It makes sense to want to indulge yourself when you are angry, but it is *right* not to rest until you've brought your anger before the Lord. As we humble ourselves and live rightly before God, we will have the defense of heaven on our side; we will have more than we need. It's only when we grasp for our-selves, demanding our rights, that God takes His hands off the situation and allows us to fend for ourselves. Consider Jesus, the One we follow. He did not consider equality with God a thing to be grasped, but laid His life down because of love (see Philippians 2:5-7). Jesus had rights, but He laid them down so that *we* could be right with God. A healthy thought life concentrates on what is right and not on self.

Gatekeeper 4—Fix your thoughts on what is pure. "God blesses those whose hearts are pure, for they will see God" (Matthew 5:8). "Your eye is a lamp for your body. A pure eye lets sunshine into your soul. But an evil eye shuts out the light and plunges you into dark-ness" (Luke 11:34). Unfortunately, even those who love us most occasionally breathe a heavy sigh because of something we say or do. And yet God, whose standard is far beyond us, always has a pure heart toward us. So instead of trying *really hard* to have a pure heart, fix your gaze on the One who is pure and true. Let your thoughts be captivated by the purity of His love. When you do this, something happens over time. When your gaze is fixed on heaven and not on what's wrong on earth, your heart becomes purified, and suddenly you become a fresh spring of hope for those who are still living earthbound lives. What you look for, you will find. Read this next verse: "Everything is pure to those whose hearts are pure. But nothing is pure to those who are corrupt and unbelieving, because their minds and consciences are defiled" (Titus 1:15). We were born for another world. We are on a journey to that Promised Land. We are here for a purpose, and we've been given very clear directives. We are not to get tangled up with the messes of dishonesty, deceit, distraction, and destruction. A healthy thought life pursues purity, and the blessing in that is that we will see more of God.

Gatekeeper 5—Fix your thoughts on what is lovely. "How lovely is your dwelling place, O LORD Almighty" (Psalm 84:1). "Hallelujah! How good it is to sing to our God, for praise is pleasant and lovely" (Psalm 147:1 HCSB). Do you want to know what is lovely? He is! Every time you catch your mind wandering, capture your thoughts and focus them on the One who loves you. Allow your mind to think about the different ways He has shown up in your life and changed it for the better. Whenever I feel depleted or distracted, I look out the window. There is something about trees and the beautiful sky that remind me of God's majesty and beauty. One Thanksgiving holiday, I went back into the woods by our house and placed ten different signs on ten different trees along with gold, foil-wrapped chocolate coins spread at the base of each tree. The signs said things like "Pause and remember the times the Lord rescued you from a difficult situation." "Pause and remember the people God has given you to love." "Pause and remember the ways God has provided for you." We silently led about four family members at a time out to the woods. We gave them a small sack and explained the journey they were about to take. Each time they would come to a tree, they were supposed to get low, pause, and remember God's faithfulness by thanking Him for each instance they could recall; and to symbolize each act of remembrance, they would place a gold coin in their sack. You cannot believe how meaningful this was. People took their time in the woods and came out with tearstained cheeks. When it was finally time to eat, we gathered round the table and emptied our sacks of gold coins. The whole table shimmered with gold foil chocolates—each representing some specific way God had come through for us. As we joined hands and prayed for our meal, Thanksgiving took on a whole new meaning that year. What's lovely to us is God. What's lovely to Him is a heart that is thankful. A healthy thought life is grateful for the lovely things God provides.

Gatekeeper 6—Fix your eyes on what is admirable. "To the faithful you show yourself faithful; to those with integrity you show integrity" (2 Samuel 22:26). "I know, my God, that you examine our hearts and rejoice when you find integrity there" (1 Chronicles 29:17). How wonderful to imagine God rejoicing when He looks in on our thought life! Imagine Him leaning over and whispering in an angel's ear, "You know, in light of what she's going through, her thoughts are sure admirable. I'm so proud of her." If for no other reason than to bring pleasure to God, it is worth it to think thoughts that are filled with security, integrity, dignity, and strength. And yet, when we do this, we do more than bring God pleasure. We affect and improve our own life. When we embrace thoughts that are admirable, we begin to make choices that follow suit. Admirable thoughts bring blessing to both heaven and earth. A healthy thought life desires that which is admirable.

Gatekeeper 7—Fix your thoughts on what is excellent. "Let heaven fill your thoughts. Do not think only about things down here on earth" (Colossians 3:2). "Don't envy sinners, but always continue to fear the LORD. For surely you have a future ahead of you; your hope will not be disappointed" (Proverbs 23:17-18). "Excellent" speaks of something that is high above the norm. Excellent thoughts are those that "look up" more often than they look down. Jesus said in Luke 12:34, "Wherever your treasure is, there your heart and thoughts will also be." Our true treasure is not to be found in the things of this world. As we believe that God never does anything halfway and that He has a plan for our lives, we will be able to think excellent thoughts when someone gets a breakthrough while we are still waiting for ours. We will be able to look past the clouds on a rainy day, knowing the blue sky is still very much in place. As we lift our gaze, our hopes, and our dreams to the author and finisher of our faith, our mind will fill with excellent thoughts. Less-than-excellent thoughts get by our gate when our eyes look to the right and left. In other words, when we start noticing what's *not* happening for us or what *is* happening for someone else or when we feel slighted and nobody apologizes or when we give a lot away and don't get any credit, we run the risk of opening the gate to many destructive thoughts unless we acknowledge those things and then quickly return our gaze to the One who won't let us down. Proverbs 17:24 says, "Sensible people keep their eyes glued on wisdom, but a fool's eyes wander to the ends of the earth." A healthy thought life is full of excellent thoughts that rise above our circumstances and hope beyond what our eyes can see.

Gatekeeper 8—Fix your thoughts on what is worthy of praise. "The heavens tell of the glory of God. The skies display his marvelous craftsmanship. Day after day they continue to speak; night after night they make him known. They speak without a sound or a word; their voice is silent in the skies; yet their message has gone out to all the earth, and their words to all the world. The sun lives in the heavens where God placed it. It bursts forth like a radiant bridegroom after his wedding. It rejoices like a great athlete eager to run the race" (Psalm 19:1-5). Do you see a theme here? God's ways and His work are far above and beyond any earthly thing. As we take our thoughts captive and make them obedient to Christ (2 Corinthians 10:5 NIV), and as we expose and remove the lies from our thought life and replace them with divine truths, *we will be transformed beyond our wildest dreams* (Romans 12:2). When we guard against ingratitude by humbly remaining thankful and when we keep our thoughts on what is right and true even if it doesn't *feel* true, we keep from *leaking* all that God has poured into us. When we make it a habit to thank God all day long for every blessing we enjoy, God joins us and the enemy doesn't dare come near us (because God is right in the midst of His praising people). If you guard your thoughts and keep them in the high place of praise, your thought life will be healthy and secure.

Precious Lord,

Transform my life by renewing the way I think. Oh, how I want to be victorious in this area! One by one, show me, Lord, what lies I have believed, where I have allowed my thoughts to wander, and where I have missed what You have for me. Raise up a new standard in my thought life so that You and the angels will have something wonderful to talk about. I want my life to honor You and bring You pleasure. Be glorified in me. Amen.

Steps Toward Health

* I will spend time with the Lord and listen to what He has to tell me about my thought life.

* I will write down the areas of my thought life that God wants to redeem. I will tuck this list in my Bible and pray regularly until I am bearing fruit in the areas of my weakness.

* I will acknowledge that though hard things happen in life, nothing happens in my heart and mind without my permission. I will confess my need for God to help me guard my thoughts.

* I will avoid the sin of comparison and statements like "I'll be okay when…" Instead, I'll embrace God's call and timing in my life. I will proclaim that He is faithful.

* I will ask the Lord to continually motivate and remind me to renew my mind each new day.

TRY THIS

* During times of fatigue, abandon all introspection and just rest. Protect yourself. This is when you are most vulnerable.

* Do *not* give your thoughts free rein during oversensitive moments. Take sides against yourself if you have to. Take your thoughts captive and make them obedient to God's truths.

* Never, ever entertain thoughts of what others might think of you. Nothing can be gained from this process, and much will be lost. Good or bad, right or wrong, they don't have all of the information. Only God does, and He loves you. Proverbs 29:25 says, "Fearing people is a dangerous trap, but to trust the LORD means safety." Do you want to feel safe with people? Fear God. Don't worry about others' gossip; just make sure

you don't gossip. Walk in the humble fear of the Lord, and you will be safe.

* Don't think about yourself for too long. C.S. Lewis called this "diseased introspection." I once pondered this thought and was shocked! I couldn't believe how often I thought about myself. Then I thought more about myself because I couldn't believe how bad I was... Do you see where this could lead? It never pays to dwell on your shortcomings, your deficits, or your downfalls. Acknowledge your need and look to Him.

* Be thankful. In your thoughts, in your prayers, out loud, and in a song, thank Him every step of the way. This will honor God and nourish your soul.

* Memorize Scripture. The Word is your weapon against the lies of the enemy, but you have to know the truth before you can refute the lies.

* Keep a tight rein on your thoughts. "If then you were raised with Christ, *seek those things which are above,* where Christ is, sitting at the right hand of God. *Set your minds on the things above,* not on things on the earth" (Colossians 3:1-2 NKJV, emphasis added). Ask for God's help, and start putting strict boundaries on your thought life. Do not let your mind go toward anything beneath faith, hope, and love. Ask for a heightened conviction in this area, and as soon as you catch yourself thinking negative thoughts, turn those thoughts into prayers that declare God's faithfulness. As you make this a practice, you'll be surprised to see even your spontaneous responses become more healthy and godly.

Balance Application

I can spend hours studying the Word of God, I can listen to countless sermons, and I can sing every day at the top of my lungs, "God is for me!" But if I don't guard my thoughts, I won't keep my joy and peace. Throughout this book, there has been an underlying theme—our lives adapt to consistent messages. When we hear something over and over, be it positive or negative, eventually it sticks with us. As we pursue a healthy thought life, we must give ourselves the gift of consistency. This may take great effort at first, but once we've blazed a new trail in our thought patterns, it will be much easier to maintain. Remember, victories are won and lost in the mind. Sin is first conceived in the mind. Our lives become distracted because our minds are distracted. It is possible to be at peace amid a storm. We just need to keep our gaze on God and His love for us.

Study Time

1. Read Romans 8:6. What does this verse mean to you? Explain.

2. Read 1 Peter 1:13.

3. Describe the areas in your life where you feel you are thinking clearly.

4. In what area of your life are things not so clear?

5. Do you exercise self-control in your thought life? Explain.

6. How can you improve in this area?

7. What blessings are you looking forward to?

8. What blessings do you forget to think about? What can you do to remind yourself to look forward with hope?

9. Read 1 Peter 1:14.

10. In what ways are you obeying God right now?

11. Are there any ways you are only giving Him partial obedience?

12. The last part of this verse tells us not to slip back into our old ways. What safeguards do you have on your life, your heart, and your mind?

13. Memorize Psalm 19:14 and Isaiah 26:3. These will help fortify your gates.

Thirteen

Spiritual Strength and Endurance

You have armed me with strength for the battle; you have subdued my enemies under my feet.

2 SAMUEL 22:40

Therefore, since we are surrounded by such a huge crowd of witnesses to the life of faith, let us strip off every weight that slows us down, especially the sin that so easily hinders our progress. And let us run with endurance the race that God has set before us.

HEBREWS 12:1

YOU'VE HEARD ME REFER BACK TO THE TIME when I was battling an illness while trying to raise three active little boys. Please allow me to revisit that season one more time. My boys were one, three, and five years old; I was in my twenties. Our house was falling apart and we had no money to fix it. We lived on very few groceries, I parented with very little strength, and our medical bills far exceeded our income. I could not see a way out. I struggled to find a purpose in it all.

I remember the day as if it were yesterday. I was sitting on our couch, which was tearing at the seams. I had holes in my jeans, and holes about to break loose in my socks. The boys were dancing to a song on *Sesame Street,* yelling and running from one end of the living room to the other. I envied their energy. My face was numb and my joints ached as I sat there on the couch. Suddenly the phone rang. I stretched the long cord down the hallway so I could hear. It was an old friend. She said, "Susie, I know we've lost touch, but I've heard of your plight and have been praying for you. I believe the Lord is using your pain to build a platform from which you will speak someday. Lean into the pain and learn all you can from it."

She shined a ray of light into my darkness. I was so buried under the heaviness of my situation that I couldn't fathom the possibility of God using this to prepare me for His purposes. But once I got a hold of the mind of Christ in my situation, the enemy couldn't as easily bully me with fear and intimidation. As soon as my friend spoke those words to me, I knew they were true. I knew that someday I would be ministering to women. In fact, my first speaking engagement took place within a year of that phone call. I was still sick, still poor, and still had holes in my jeans, but I packed up my little ones and went to speak to a mom's group about how I was keeping my faith during such a time of struggle.

Things got worse before they got better, and I battled many things along the way, but I had in my heart a sense of calling from the Lord. I decided I would trust His voice more than the messages my circumstances were sending me. I received great inspiration from heroes of the Bible like Joseph and Job.

Joseph had a calling on his life. God put a dream in his heart. But he, like me, didn't have the maturity to handle it in his younger years. God allowed incredible injustice and heartache to take place in his life that would prepare him to rule with justice and kindness. With every unjust situation, Joseph yielded, trusted, and was teachable, and in every case he rose to a leadership role. Joseph's situation is described in Psalm 105:16-22. The passage says that God sent him ahead, though it appeared he'd been left behind. You see, God is always thinking ahead and preparing us to meet needs that are further down the road. Joseph was sold into slavery, falsely accused, and sent to prison. He learned patience, humility, and obedience through the things he suffered. Jesus did too. "Even though Jesus was God's Son, he learned obedience from the things he suffered" (Hebrews 5:8).

We, too, will learn patience, humility, and obedience through the things we suffer. Author, pastor, and counselor Mark Spencer serves on my church's advisory board. Whenever he counsels people who are struggling through heavy circumstances, he first seeks God and asks Him the question, "Is it a sin or a test?" Some of the pain we go through we bring upon ourselves; other times God simply allows hard times to strengthen us. This is what's wonderful about God, though. Even *if* our struggle is because of sin, if we confess it before Him, He will, in His divine wisdom, use the consequences to do a beautiful, miraculous work in us.

It's important to note that we can lengthen the days of our struggle by our own lack of faith. The Israelites took 40 years to complete a journey that should have taken them about a week. One commentary explained that their wandering through the desert was a consequence of their rebellious fears. Think about that. Fear can be rebellious. While God is merciful and understands when we are afraid, we must understand that if we cling too tightly to our fears, it is an affront to His love and faithfulness. "Perfect love casts out fear" (1 John 4:18 NKJV).

"The people *refused* to enter the pleasant land, *for they wouldn't believe his promise to care for them. Instead, they grumbled in their tents* and *refused to obey the* LORD" (Psalm 106:24-25, emphasis added). The Israelites' journey parallels our journey. They were not made for captivity. They were made to live free. *We are not made for captivity. We are made to live free.* "For you, dear friends, have been called to live in freedom—not freedom to satisfy your sinful nature, but freedom to serve one another in love" (Galatians 5:13). Everything that binds us, ties us up, and makes us insecure is based on a lie. Oswald Chambers wrote, "We have an incredible capacity for God, but sin, wrong thinking, and unbelief keep us from Him."[1] As we learn to believe that everything that comes our way serves a higher purpose, our faith will grow along with our tenacity to hang in there when things get tough.

Free to Dream

Do you have a dream in your heart? At my engagements I sometimes ask women to tell me what dreams are hiding inside. All too often they shrink back and sheepishly share something that seems way out of their reach. Did you know that every one of us is called to a dream that is bigger than ourselves? Sadly, most people never do anything about their dream because of fear, lack of faith, or little desire to leave their comfort zone. But there are those who listen to that inner voice, dare to trust in the God of big dreams, and venture out. However, before taking hold of the prize, they sometimes will enter a time of humbling preparation, inner strengthening, and character refining.

As you look carefully at the components of spiritual strength and endurance, it is important to be thinking about the direction in your life. God wants to lead you somewhere. He wants you to step out in faith. He wants to multiply your gifts *and* their impact. He wants to surprise you by showing up in impossible situations. He has a specific plan and purpose that He's wired you for. If you haven't done this yet, go before Him and get a sense of what that ultimate calling might be. "'For I know the plans I have for you,' says the LORD. 'They are plans for good and not for disaster, to give you a future and a hope'" (Jeremiah 29:11).

As we look beyond our circumstances with the hope and the knowledge that God is up to something, our struggles are easier to bear. When we know *and believe* that our hard times are working in us something wonderful, those struggles will not have the power to wound and disillusion us the way they used to.

Spiritual Strength Training

In the first half of this book, we addressed physical strength. We learned that when we lift properly, our body gets stronger and our capacity to lift heavier weight without injury increases. It's the same in our spiritual lives. God, in His grace, filters through His hands measured trials. He knows our frame (Psalm 103:14 NKJV). He knows how much we can handle, and He fits us with a yoke that's just right for us. "For my yoke fits perfectly, and the burden I give you is light" (Matthew 11:30).

I know that doesn't always feel true. It certainly didn't for me. Back in my days of back-to-back crises, I would often throw my head back and yell out, "Lord, I think you have me mixed up with Susie Larson in Cincinnati, because this is far more than I can handle!"

I eventually realized that much of the weight that was crushing me was self-induced; it came from my own lack of faith, my fear, and my desire to have what *I* wanted more than what God wanted for me. Once I submitted my will to Him, peace came in and I was no longer bent beneath my load.

Here are a few things to remember about spiritual strength training.

Heavy things make us stronger. "Search for the LORD and for his strength, and keep on searching" (1 Chronicles 16:11). God allows completely painful circumstances and unjust people to trip us up and weigh us down. But it is in the shifting of our weight and the digging deep for strength that we learn love and grace. This is where we gain the spiritual muscle to weather the storm. We must refuse weights of guilt, fear, shame, and condemnation, for they are not from God. Anger, selfishness, and unforgiveness are also weights that slow us down. In the first half of the book I said that you can get your body to do almost anything as long as you "ask nicely" and take a step at a time. Well, the way we ask nicely in the spiritual realm is to rid our lives of weights that Jesus died for and carry only what He asks us to. Our power and our strength come from God. We can stand up under our load when we look for Him and find Him *in* our struggle...and then *believe* what He says.

Resistance in life isn't without its purpose. "In your strength I can crush an army; with my God I can scale any wall" (Psalm 18:29). Every one of us will face battles in life. Sometimes God allows "enemies" in our land to teach us how to battle against the true enemy of our soul. But we do not battle as the world does. We battle hatred with love, offense with forgiveness, impatience with kindness, and pride with humility. We cannot hide our heads in the sand in hopes that no evil, betrayal, or injustice will darken our doorstep. They will, and we must be armed ahead of time with such an overwhelming sense of the love of God that we are quickly able to put evil under our feet and walk on in love. If we are not prepared, we will engage in a battle on a level we cannot win. Our only defense is Christ. "For every child of God defeats this evil world by trusting Christ to give the victory. And the ones who win this battle against the world are the ones who believe that Jesus is the Son of God" (1 John 5:4-5). Whatever army rises up against us, whatever wall stands in our way, God has given us strength to overcome it. Sometimes He will allow us a time of straining and pushing against something that will not budge, and then suddenly one day we will step back and realize that in all of our resisting against the obstacle, we've gained the spiritual muscle to go over it! "Such people will not be overcome by evil circumstances. Those who are righteous will be long remembered. They do not fear bad news; they confidently trust the LORD to care for them. They are confident and fearless and can face their foes triumphantly" (Psalm 112:6-8).

Resistance breaks down old limitations and builds up a new threshold. "The war between the house of Saul and the house of David dragged on and on. The longer it went on the stronger David became, with the house of Saul getting weaker" (2 Samuel 3:1 MSG). This is a critical point. Both David and Saul were involved in the *same* fight, but over time one grew in strength while the other grew weaker. David walked humbly in the fear of the Lord. He fought the battles God called him to. He obeyed God and repented when he sinned. Saul, on the other hand, operated out of greed, lust for power, jealousy, and insecurity. He lost sight of the bigger picture and exhausted himself trying to rescue his sense of self-worth.

Women battle over these same issues. We grab for what we want, we either get too big or too small when someone threatens us, and we get good at pointing out flaws in others while magnifying the things that we do well. God help us! When we come to a place of such assurance in the Lord that we clearly see insecurity, jealousy, and greed as things that diminish strength, we will be quicker to put those things under our feet. As we walk in humble fear of the Lord, repent when we sin, and fervently battle against attitudes and responses that weaken our spiritual muscle and lessen our love, over time we will find ourselves stronger, more steadfast, and unafraid of the future. "She is clothed with strength and dignity, and she laughs with no fear of the future" (Proverbs 31:25).

Atrophy. "To those who are open to my teaching, more understanding will be given, and they will have an abundance of knowledge. But to those who are not listening, even what they have will be taken away from them" (Matthew 13:12). Spiritual atrophy happens when we take a break from the things of God. If we put off our walk of faith for some other day, we will eventually become soft and weak. Every morning we wake up to fresh mercies and a chance to start again. Every day we're given opportunity to serve Him well and faithfully use our gifts. Today we have the chance to learn more about Jesus, to spend more time in His presence, develop the gifts He has given us, and to reach out to those who don't know Him. Those who lived for Him, who daily brought their sins and frailties to the cross, who spent their gifts on a lost and dying world, and who kept heaven busy with countless prayers of faith...they will be able to look into their Savior's eyes and hear Him say, "Well done, my good and faithful servant" (Matthew 25:23).

Seek Him now. Draw all of your strength from Him. Give yourself and your gifts away with the holy expectation that He will replenish you. Use what He's given you. Ask forgiveness when you sin. Keep heaven busy with your prayers. Take hold of all that's been taken hold for you, and more will be given. Keep your spiritual muscles working and stretching.

Keep the bigger picture in mind. "Don't shuffle along, eyes to the ground, absorbed with the things right in front of you. Look up, and be alert to what is going on around Christ—that's where the action is. See things from his perspective" (Colossians 3:2 MSG). Nothing is impossible with God, and overwhelming victory belongs to us who belong to Him (see Romans 8:37).

Here is a story to illustrate my point. Matthew 14 describes a time when Jesus was in the hills praying and His disciples were on a boat, battling a great storm. Jesus walked out on the water and assured them it would be okay. "Peter called to him, 'Lord, if it's really you, tell me to come to you by walking on the water'" (verse 28). 'Alright, come,' Jesus said" (verse 29). First of all, notice how Peter did not attempt the impossible without the call and the permission of his Lord. That is very important for us to remember. (Now, back to the story.) The Bible then says that Peter *went over the boat, and walked on the water.* Imagine that! He took a risk when God called him, and he experienced the thrill of stepping out in faith with Jesus. But read the next verse closely. "But when he *looked around* at the *high waves, he was terrified* and *began to sink*" (Matthew 14:30, emphasis added). He looked too long at what was rising up against him. He lost sight of Jesus right in front of him, and what happened? He was weighed down by his own fear. There is no shame in being afraid as long as we know where to turn with our fear. Let's look at Peter's quick response: "'Save me, Lord!' he shouted" (Matthew 14:30) and at Jesus' response: "Instantly Jesus reached out his hand and grabbed him. 'You don't have much faith,' Jesus said. 'Why did you doubt me?'" (Matthew 14:31). Jesus is always "instantly" there for us. At the same time, He is always calling us to a higher perspective. Make it a habit to look at your life and your situation with God in mind every day.

Precious Lord,

You are the strength of my heart. May I never be afraid of the battles life promises. Instead, may I rise up every day with a fresh awareness of Your power within me. Help me to face my foes with a courageous and humble heart. More than anything, I ask that You keep my love alive. It is far too easy to let go of love when hard times press in; and yet this is when love is most needed. I long to stand strong when the storms hit. I want to keep my eyes on You when the waves get bigger than me. Everything I need is found in You. Keep me close, Lord. Amen.

Steps Toward Health

- I will pause and remember the times God has been faithful. I will allow these memories to strengthen my faith.

- I will ask God for a fresh perspective on the things that are currently pressing in on me.

- I will take steps to strengthen my "spiritual muscle" by developing a gift God has given me.

- I will forgive whoever may be causing me pain or discomfort. I will seek God for help in this.

- I will refuse to let my circumstances define me. I will look to Jesus and allow Him to put fresh hope and a dream in my heart.

- I will not give up when times of preparation and testing come.

TRY THIS

* Write down the thing that is currently pressing in on you. What's at risk right now (honor, reputation, provision, security, friendships, health)? Using a concordance, find a corresponding Scripture and memorize it. For instance, if you are feeling humiliated, memorize Psalm 62:7: "My salvation and my honor come from God alone. He is my refuge, a rock where no enemy can reach me."

* Pay attention to your thoughts and your gaze. Spend more time thinking about God's love and faithfulness than your current situation. You'll keep your peace by looking at Him. "You will keep in perfect peace all who trust in you, whose thoughts are fixed on you!" (Isaiah 26:3).

* Keep short accounts with your sin. Ask God for forgiveness the minute you realize you have said or done something you shouldn't. It is especially during turbulent times that we are vulnerable to fall or fail. If we allow pride or ignorance to keep us from admitting when we are wrong, we venture out into deep waters without Jesus by our side. (Note: His love goes with us everywhere, even to the depths of the sea, but if we refuse to humble ourselves, He will allow us to fall into our own sin. See Proverbs 16:18.) We will be strengthened in our struggles when we humbly stand against the sin that so easily ensnares us. Jesus draws near to the humble in heart, but He actually distances Himself from the proud. "Though the LORD is great, he cares for the humble, but he keeps his distance from the proud" (Psalm 138:6).

* Pay attention to the growth process and be encouraged. As we walk closely with the Lord and do what He says, we will gain

spiritual health and strength. Make it a practice to notice how able you are to carry something that would have put you under a year ago. Amid all of our daily battles and struggles, we must take time to remember and be encouraged by our victories.

Balance Application

Spiritually speaking, heavy things make us stronger if we allow them to. No matter who we are, we will face battles in this life. But if we choose to take God at His word and trust Him in the hard times, we will find our spiritual lives strengthened beyond belief. As we remember that He works everything together for our good (Romans 8:28), we will have the courage to walk through storms that threaten to sweep us away. When we keep our feet firmly planted on the Rock of our Salvation (see Psalm 95:1), the raging waters will only prove to us that He is sufficient. Before attempting the impossible, we will wait for the call of God, we will expect resistance, and then choose to view it as preparation. We will keep our eyes on Jesus, knowing He is faithful. When hard times press in, our faith can grow and our love can increase; but for that to happen we must first ask this question: Is my goal to be delivered from my discomfort or to be perfected in love? If my heart is set on the Lord and His purifying work in my life, I will grow indeed (see 2 Thessalonians 1:3-4). On the hard days, we will hold our ground, on the better days, we will take more ground. We won't give up what we've already gained.

Study Time

1. Read Romans 8:31. Who or what seems to be against you right now? Is it any match for God? Pause for a moment, and reflect on the fact that God is *for* you.

2. Read Romans 8:32. Think about what love cost our heavenly Father. Think about all He has provided for us. Why do you suppose it is difficult to believe that He will withhold no good thing from us (see Psalm 84:11)? Stop and pray right now about any barriers to your faith.

3. Read Romans 8:33-34. Read it again. Read this every time someone rises up against you. Is there someone in your life who has intimidated or accused you? How much time have you given to thinking about it? Confess any sin you may have committed, apologize for any way you might be wrong, read the verse again, and trust Him to deliver you.

4. Read Romans 8:35-36. *Can* anything separate us from His love? *Does* it mean He doesn't love us when resistance comes our way? *Will* we continue to encounter trials during our journey on earth? Write down what you *know* to be true.

5. Read Romans 8:37. In spite of our struggles, how do we secure a victory? How can you personally apply this promise?

6. Read Romans 8:38-39. Read it again. This time, read it out loud and personalize it. Replace "us" with "me." Pay attention to what you are reading. Hear the love, the strength, and the passion behind those words. Allow this

powerful promise to fill you up and strengthen you. This would be a great passage to memorize.

7. Take a moment and write down all of the things that are pressing you (on separate sheets of paper). One by one, hold them up and confess out loud, "Lord, I have worried about _____ for too long. I have decided to trust You today with the outcome. From now on, I will spend my time focusing on Your faithfulness." Take your time, get through each piece of paper, and then throw them in the garbage, burn them in a bonfire, or stick them to a cross. This outward, symbolic gesture serves the enemy notice and proclaims, "I will no longer look at my fears. I will look to Jesus instead!"

8. Read 2 Corinthians 12:9-10. Describe a time when you saw God's power shine through your weakness. Remember this principle: When we are weakest, He is most strong. Don't hide your weaknesses. Bring them before the Lord and say, "Father, here is another area where I need Your grace. Thank You for Your grace."

9. Read 2 Corinthians 6:1-10.

10. Read it again. Allow this passage to challenge you, inspire you, and give you perspective. Today, approximately one Christian every three minutes is martyred for their faith. Pause and pray for your own situation as well as for your suffering brothers and sisters all over the world.

Fourteen
Spiritual "Cardio"

*Therefore as you have received Christ Jesus
the Lord, walk in Him, rooted and built up in
Him and established in the faith, just as you
were taught, and overflowing with thankfulness.*

COLOSSIANS 2:6-7 HCSB

*May the Lord bring you into an ever deeper
understanding of the love of God and the
endurance that comes from Christ.*

2 THESSALONIANS 3:5

MORE THAN 20 YEARS AGO, I WAS RIDING IN AN old van with several other college students. We were making our way home for a
much-needed break. While the other students enjoyed banter back
and forth, I was lost in a Watchman Nee book. I cannot remember
the title, but I was in a world of my own. Every once in a while I
would put the book over my heart, close my eyes, and silently pray
about something I had read. This godly man had profound things to
say, and I wanted all of them to fully nourish my soul.

Again, I wish I could remember the title of the book, because then I could find the passage that rocked my world and share it with you. But I will tell you this. After reading a certain chapter, I was overcome with a deeper understanding of how shallow I was. I again put the book to my heart, and within seconds I saw my life flash before my eyes. Like a fast-moving reel, the frames of my life passed before me, showing me that most everything I had ever done had been done with *me* in mind. Even acts of service were done to rescue my sense of self-worth or to look good or so that someone wouldn't be upset with me.

Only once in a while, very rarely, in fact, did the frame slow down enough to show me a time when I had served or given or loved simply because it was what God wanted me to do. At the time it felt sacrificial, but sitting there in that dumpy old van, in a deep state of prayer, I saw from heaven's perspective the richness and the value behind an act done simply for the sake of love.

The revelation of my impure motives became clearer, and my hand went over my mouth. I did not want to speak for fear that my next words or actions would spring from a selfish heart. For the rest of the ride I kept my eyes closed and prayed for forgiveness and a cleansing of my heart. I could barely speak for the next three days. Thankfully, being home from college, I could really lean into this time. I cried in my room. I cried out on the deck. I went for a run and cried with every step I took. Honestly, it felt good and very cleansing. It wasn't that I was under condemnation; it's more that my heart was broken over my level of selfishness. Every time God shows me a new level of my selfishness, I gain a deeper appreciation of what I've been forgiven. I also become more passionately thankful for a sacrifice that covered my sin before I was even aware of its implications.

For those three days, I spent extensive amounts of time examining my heart and bringing my need before the Lord, kneeling in humility and awe that the God of the universe would even consider having me for a friend. The following verses and quote by Henry Edward Manning capture my thoughts perfectly:

> When I look at the night sky and see the work of your fingers—the moon and the stars you have set in place—what are mortals that you should think of us, mere humans that you should care for us? For you made us only a little lower than God, and you crowned us with glory and honor (Psalm 8:3-5).

> Wheresoever we be, whatsoever we are doing, in all our work, in our busy daily life, in all schemes and undertakings, in public trust, and in private retreats, He is with us, and all we do is spread before Him. Do it, then, as to the Lord. Let the thought of His eye unseen be the motive of your acts and words. Do nothing you would not have Him see. Say nothing which you would not have said before His visible presence. This is to do all in His name.[1]

The verse at the beginning of this chapter (Colossians 2:6) tells us that since we have received Christ, we are to *walk in Him*. We lose our strength when we walk *away* from truths; truths that cost Christ everything to deliver to us. Jesus is literally the air we breathe. He is the oxygen that fuels us to do things we could never otherwise do. He defines us, and we must take hold of our value in Him. If we believe we have something to prove, we will serve to get, not to give. If we believe we need more attention than we're getting, we will serve to get, not to give. If we believe we lack worth, we will serve to get, not to give. That's not to say we should sit and wait until we're full before we go out and give what's been deposited in us away. What we need, though, is to daily, moment by moment, offer ourselves up to God and ask Him to search our hearts for any impure motives, to bring us truth where we believe a lie, and to give us strength where we are weak.

When we allow God to deal with and purify our inner motives, our service to Him will have a much greater impact and be far more nourishing to a starving world than service (and gifts) given with mixed motives. Serving out of emptiness will indeed feed some; but serving from fullness will feed many more. In John 15:16, Jesus appoints us to go and "produce fruit that will last." He also reminds us that when we stay connected to Him, feeding from the love and the strength He gives, we will accomplish much. "Yes, I am the vine; you are the branches. Those who remain in me, and I in them, will produce much fruit. For apart from me you can do nothing" (John 15:5).

Why does He need to tell us to remain? Because the current of sin, selfishness, and wrong thinking threatens to sweep us away. Every day the enemy sends us messages in many different ways, all in the hope to make us second-guess ourselves, lose our footing, and be swept from the Rock of our salvation. How do we remain in Him? We daily confess our needs, our weaknesses, our hopes, and our dreams. We nourish ourselves on the Word of truth, and we listen to the Holy Spirit say, "This is the way; walk in it" (Isaiah 30:21 NIV).

In the first half of the book, I wrote this statement: At the heart of true, lasting balance is the ability to read your health and your circumstances and then adjust accordingly. This is especially true in the spiritual realm. As you walk more closely with the Lord, you will have a heightened sense of your need. You'll know when it is best to step out and take a risk and serve, and when it is best to pull back and get your cup full once again. Ideally, you will make these adjustments daily or at least weekly. If you suddenly feel that your cup is empty and your responses reflect your lack of fullness, use your time wisely and do what you can to get before the Lord. He may just give you a verse or a moment of clarity. He may simply infuse you with energy to finish your day. You may find that at other times you are overflowing with strength. Be prepared. God will provide opportunities for you to share your fullness with others.

As you gear up to take your spiritual health to another level, here are a few things to keep in mind.

Tangible Tips as You Prepare for Spiritual Exercise

Take an honest assessment. Assess where you are in your spiritual health *and* your stage of life. While it is good to dream about where you want the Lord to take you, it is for your own protection that you also honestly look at every area of your life. Do you have young children? Do you have a rebellious child who requires more of your time? Are you caring for aging parents? How about your "inner cup"? Is it half full, is it empty, is it overflowing? Listen closely and God will tell you daily what you have time for: when to run, when to rest, when to serve, and when to be served. We need Him every hour. Some seasons are filled with grace, while others require that both our arms and legs be clinging to the Vine simply to hold our ground. When we get used to paying attention to what our souls need, we will more quickly bring ourselves to our Source of strength. Our need and our availability will vary throughout the days, weeks, months, and seasons of life. Pay attention to where you are. This will help you maintain a life of balance.

Ask nicely. Remember this tip from the chapter on physical health? When you take small steps and incorporate disciplines one at a time, you can improve your life in ways you cannot even imagine. Be content to start where you need to. Resist the temptation to look around at where anyone else is in their pursuit of God and their service to Him. Walk, lift, and stretch just beyond what is comfortable for you. In other words, God will call you to carry certain things and He will lead you further than you can imagine, but He does so one step at a time. Give yourself permission to be a work in progress. We all are. Just as no one could jump into your household and run it the way you do, you cannot jump into a fully developed calling without first being trained and prepared for it. Embrace the process. The journey is as sacred as the destination.

Leave the comfort zone. You are probably sick of hearing this by now, but that means you will remember it: *In order to grow, we must push beyond what is comfortable.* When God asks us to, we must be willing to take risks. To risk is to take the chance of failure, humiliation, or embarrassment. To risk is to dig deep and do something that would be easier left undone. To risk is to love or give something away, knowing your love may not be reciprocated. In light of this, think of all the ways Jesus took risks with us. He was willing to risk His reputation, His respectability, and His comfort, knowing He would die without many even acknowledging His gift, and yet He thought of you and me. His love for us compelled Him to take a gigantic risk so His kingdom would be enlarged. We, too, will be called on to take risks that will seem beyond us. But He will be with us every step of the way.

Understand endurance vs. change. Know when God is calling you to press on and when He is telling you to let go. The thing you are doing might have been God's plan to begin with, but maybe now He is moving in a totally different direction and you must follow.

Sometimes we stick it out and hang in there with something that God is no longer blessing or calling us to. The grace for the task lifts and the "thing" begins to feel heavier and heavier. This is where some make the mistake of thinking it noble and martyr-like to hang in there, even though it is killing their joy, strength, and perspective. There seems to be a window of time God provides to get out, and *not* to do so eventually becomes disobedience through lack of faith. Those who stay after the window has closed often experience a level of burnout so severe that they never fully recover from it.

On the other hand, sometimes the Lord allows everything around you to go dry, but still there's the seed of faith, the call in your heart, the promise in His Word that He will take your offering and multiply it for His kingdom. You *must* hang in there in such cases. Many leave just before their breakthrough arrives. It is important to be able to differentiate between the two. Seek the Lord in these matters, and also seek wise counsel. The Holy Spirit will help you know whether to let go or hang on.

Don't give up what you've gained. "We must be sure to obey the truth we have learned already" (Philippians 3:16). Remember this point? It is much harder to get something back than it is to maintain it. Use what God has given you. Hang on to the disciplines you already have. Use your gifts and guard the ground you have gained in your walk of faith. Think about relationships, good habits, and skills. In every area of life are examples of things that require our attention or we will eventually lose them. How do we give up what we've gained? A little at a time. We make little allowances here and there, and, at first, suffer no consequences. But just as we mentioned in the first section, our lives will respond to the most consistent message. If every message we send is inconsistent, a disjointed, unfocused, and possibly sinful life will eventually result. In her book *Something More*, Catherine Marshall writes:

> Usually we think we deserve a "little fun" by a fling into sinning when life has handed us some injustice or when we have stuck faithfully through some protracted trial. A degree of self-pity joins the blown-up pride of our self-congratulation of having been so patient and reliable. Many of us have found out to our sorrow what a deadly brew this is. Our eyes are completely off Christ and on ourselves. Out of this little mess Satan has worked some great triumphs.[2]

Take more ground on the good days. You've also heard this concept several times, but when you have strength to give, help someone. When you have some extra time, turn it into a Sabbath moment and pray. Keep heaven busy with your prayers. When you find yourself in a season of ease, dig into the Word of God. Study, learn, pray, and serve Him with all the strength He provides. When you are enduring a storm, *know* that the Lord is loving and true and don't stop looking for Him. Soon you will find Him, and He will reward your faith. In every season make the most of every opportunity. "So be careful how you live, not as fools but as those who are wise. Make the most of every opportunity for doing good in these evil days" (Ephesians 5:15-16). One more note on this point. When the Old Testament kings who feared the Lord experienced a time of favor, they often fortified their cities. They strengthened their gates. When you are in a time of ease, tackle your areas of weakness. Bring them before the Lord and continue to do so until they become strengths. Is it time, money, relationships? Fortify your life.

It takes energy to make energy. We learned in the first half of the book that, to improve our physical health and strength and increase our energy level, we *have* to work out even when we don't feel like it. It's the same with our spiritual lives. At first, more times than not, we won't *feel* like being kind when we're irritable. We won't *feel* like giving to someone who doesn't deserve it. We won't *feel* like making a commitment to serve in a way that will cost us. But every time we die to our selfishness that we may live more like Christ, God will provide increased strength to do the thing that seems way beyond us. As we step out, Jesus steps in. In her wonderful book *Come Away My Beloved,* Frances J. Roberts writes: "Where there is the activity of the Almighty, there are forces of Life continually working to produce within thee a measure of the life and health and strength which are in Him."[3]

There is no limit to what God can do through a trusting, yielded heart. As we lay ourselves down, every single day, and open our hearts to what He has to say (and then do quickly what He asks us to), He will trust us more and more with the honor of serving Him in miraculous, awesome ways. With every year that passes of walking faithfully with the Lord, we will be able to look back in awe of the ways He showed up, moved mountains, and used such imperfect souls to do His work. Each year as we press on in His name, both in crisis and in times of favor, we will gain ground and spiritual endurance. Read the following quote by Rick Joyner:

> The athlete's endurance does not increase until he reaches the previous limit of his endurance and overtakes it. The same is true of our spiritual endurance. We can testify with Paul: "I can do all things through Him who strengthens me" (Philippians 4:13). In Christ we can never say "can't" to what He has called us to do. We

can say that we "will not" or "did not," but we can never say that we "can not." He has given us *His* strength.[4]

Practice good posture. As I mentioned before, it wears on our physical frame to slouch and hang our head. When we stand tall, our core strength improves. Plus, we look healthier and more confident. This is even more important spiritually speaking. We must not cower, hang our head, or second-guess our value. We have to remember who we are and *whose* we are. If there is anything in our heart that would cause us to hang our head, we need to put this book down right now, confess it, and spend a moment in God's presence, allowing His Spirit to cleanse us from every wrong. Have you read this verse lately? "But if we confess our sins to him, he is faithful and just to forgive us and to cleanse us from every wrong" (1 John 1:9). You have every reason to walk with a holy confidence that declares, "I belong to Him" and a humble dependence that proclaims, "I have nothing apart from Him." Practice good spiritual posture every single day.

Listen to your body. If we are in a season where we are able to give a lot away, we especially need to pay attention to our need for nourishment and rest. If we go too long emphasizing one lever (output), at the expense of the others, we will throw our lives and relationships out of whack. Conversely, if we are in a crisis season where we are taking in more than giving out, we will have certain days where we are stronger than usual. On those days, don't be surprised if the opportunity pops up to bless someone else. Those sacred moments of blessing others amid our own struggle strengthen us for His service.

Practice spiritual flexibility. "We can make our plans, but the LORD determines our steps" (Proverbs 16:9). Before I ever had the courage to write my first book, I asked God to confirm that this was His plan. (I was such a woman of faith, I only asked for confirmation about 13 times.) Finally, when I knew it was His plan for me to write *Mercy in the Wilderness,* I sat down at my computer. And I sat. Absolutely nothing was coming to me, so I prayed, "Lord?" His whisper came quickly across my heart. *Your neighbor needs you.* Being the spiritual giant that I am, I replied, "Huh?" Again, that still, small voice prompted me to go to my neighbor's house. She opened the door with tear-filled eyes and asked, "How did you know?" After a sweet time of sharing and praying, I headed back home. The Lord made it clear that I must always be listening, always be flexible, and always be available to do what He asks me to. Even when we have received clear direction from the Lord, we must never go on autopilot or assume the road will be a straight one. Often, while giving us the vision to go west, the Lord takes us east.

He also gets to decide if the service we perform seems beyond us or beneath us, and we will always be asked to do both no matter what season we are in. This helps to remind us who is in charge and whom we serve. We must be careful to remember during times of favor and success that no service is beneath us, and if we think it is, we have wandered away from the heart of Christ. In our seasons of crisis and seeming defeat, we must not look down or look away with self-doubt. We must look up and receive the strength He provides and accomplish what He wills as He leads. If we remain teachable and flexible, and understand that the Lord has the right to change courses and plans any time He wishes, we will be prepared to move when He does. "Be dressed for service and well prepared" (Luke 12:35).

Every yes is three-dimensional. As easy as it is to say, "Yes, I'll do that. Of course I'll take care of that. Sure. I don't mind doing that," we must remember that with each yes we offer comes with it a commitment of time, energy, and space. When our yeses pile up, we find ourselves stressed-out and overwhelmed. This has a direct effect on our health and the quality of our life. It is good to say yes once in a while; it is even better to pause, pray, look at our schedule, and talk with our spouse or a good friend before committing our time. Oswald Chambers once wrote, "The good is always the enemy of the best."[5] There are a million good things we could do with our time; but our lives will be much more peaceful and powerful when we do the *best* things God has called us to.

Don't go through the motions. We serve a living, loving, holy, and powerful God. If we have given our lives to Christ, they do not belong to us anymore. He gets to decide when to give things to us, when to take them away, where we go, and whom we bless. If we get in a mode where our walk of faith and our service to Him becomes rote, it means we have lost sight of our first love. God's love is what fuels us and gives us passion. If we've lost our passion, it's because we've lost sight of His love. If this is true for you, go back and read chapters 9 and 10. Remember again how much Jesus enjoys you and wants to fill you with every good thing. Allow your thoughts to be flooded with the fact that He loves you and has a specific plan for your life. Get back to the most basic and important fact in the world: *You are the object of His love.* You are not summed up by what you do; you are defined as someone He enjoys. Let that thought fuel you and excite you to get back out there and represent Christ to a lost and dying world.

When a man asked Jesus what he must do to be saved, Jesus replied, "That you love the Lord your God with all your passion and prayer and muscle and intelligence—and that you love your neighbor as well as you do yourself" (Luke 10:27 MSG). Start there. Love yourself. Love your next-door neighbor. Love your children. Love your husband. Love those around you and be kind to those who irritate you. If you take these few simple steps of love, you will change the world.

One more note on this point. I mentioned in the first section that the more you invest and apply yourself to each exercise, the more benefits you will receive. Again, it's the same in our spiritual lives, but in this case, the benefits we receive are far more significant because they affect things in this life *and* in the life to come. The person who prepares for church the night before by turning off the TV, putting praise music on, praying for their pastor and worship team, and asking God to prepare their own heart for what He has to say will get far more out of the service than someone who stays out too late the night before, wakes up late, and shows up with a foggy brain only to be spoon fed by their pastor. Try it once. If you're about to go to a concert or to a Bible study or to church or to visit a friend, do a little investing beforehand. On the nights your kids have activities at church, fast and pray that day for them and for those teaching them. There is an inexhaustible supply of blessings in heaven, and God longs for us to reach up and open a trap door to His storehouse.

God's Saving Work

Meditate on the following verse. Take your time reading it and allow it to nourish, convict, and inspire you. How can we be even more careful to put into action God's powerful, holy, and supernatural saving work in our lives? How can we obey Him with an even deeper sense of reverence and awe? We do so by embracing and believing that He *is* working in us, changing us, and giving us the desire *and the power* to do the impossible. We are more than conquerors when we walk closely with the Father.

> You must be even more careful to put into action God's saving work in your lives, obeying God with deep reverence and fear. For God is working in you, giving you the desire to obey him and the power to do what pleases him (Philippians 2:12-13).

Precious Lord,

You are everything to me. Fill me up with more of You. Forgive me for the countless times I gave or served only to get something in return. All I could ever need is found in You. You are the Source of life and every insecurity is swallowed up in Your love. Oh, how I want to know more and more of that love! I want to fulfill every last thing You created me for. Increase my faith, increase my love, and increase my capacity to know You more. Show me where I am called to serve, and help me lay down the things I am not called to. I long to live a life that counts for something so much bigger than myself. You have provided all I need to accomplish more than I can imagine. If I am doing too much, help me to simplify my life. Help me to do less and do it more powerfully. If I am not doing enough, give me a passion for Your kingdom. Nothing matters more than living life for You. Thank You, Jesus. Amen.

Steps Toward Health

- No matter where I think I am at, I will pause to ask God to show me what He sees.

- I will bring my life and my schedule before the Lord and ask Him to inspire, convict, and encourage me where I need it.

- I will embrace the promise that no matter where I am, Jesus thoroughly loves and enjoys me. He cheers for me when I get it right and aches for me when I get it wrong.

- I will *practice* good spiritual posture daily by remembering who I am and whose I am. Soon it will become instinctive for me to stand strong in all seasons.

- As I simplify my life and begin to enjoy room to breathe, I will be open, available, and flexible for whatever God calls me to. I won't sigh when my plans are interrupted. I will look at new plans as a divine redirection of my day.

TRY THIS

- Memorize these two verses: "Search me, O God, and know my heart; test me and know my thoughts. Point out anything in me that offends you, and lead me along the path of everlasting life" (Psalm 139:23-24).

- Pray these verses every morning. Pray these verses before you make a commitment. Pray these verses the minute you lose your peace. When you stay close to the Source, you'll know right away which choices, which words, and which commitments threaten to lure you away from your first love and passion.

- Remember, kids always come before ministry, and husbands before kids.

- Before you commit to anything, always ask yourself why you are doing it and whom you are trying to serve.

- Never say yes right away. Think, pray, look at your schedule, and, if applicable, talk to your spouse.

- Seek peace and pursue it...always (see Psalm 34:14).

- Intentionally choose to love those closest to you in a more active way than you normally do. (Be creative!)

- Always look for the sacred moments throughout the day... they are there for the taking.

- Remember that His mercies are new every morning and His faithfulness is great (Lamentations 3:22-23 NKJV).

- At the end of each day, as you lay your head on the pillow, make sure you've not taken any accounts against others to bed with you. Make sure you have left them at the cross of forgiveness and have become a friend to grace again.

- We bring pleasure to God when we live by faith. Ask Him, "Lord, what would You have me believe You for right now? Change in my marriage, virtue in my children, blessing in our schools, revival in our church? How do You want to expand Your kingdom through me?" Plant that mustard seed of faith in your heart, water it with prayer and a holy expectation, and then see what happens.

Balance Application

To do what God has called you to will at times seem beyond you and other times beneath you. If you want to learn more about the focus and courage it takes to make an impact in your world, read about Noah and Nehemiah. God wants to accomplish life- and world-changing feats through you as well. Wait on Him and get your marching orders from Him. "A wise woman builds her house, a foolish woman tears hers down with her own hands" Proverbs 14:1.) Build with your eyes on Jesus and your heart set on obeying Him. Don't seek to be understood but to understand the Lord's plan and His love for all people. Seek to understand where those who don't understand you are coming from. Do what He's called you to; no more, no less. Be brave in your calling. Refuse bitterness and pettiness. Take care of yourself so you won't fall into the temptation of blaming others. Take seriously the calling on your life and nurture all God has given you to accomplish it. Embrace the life you have in Christ. It is a priceless gift.

Study Time

1. Read Luke 12:22-24. What cares of life most occupy your thoughts?

2. Read Luke 12:25-29. What helps you not to worry? Write it down. Jesus commands us not to worry because He knows that when we worry, we are most vulnerable to the schemes of the enemy. That is when we are most easily led astray, seduced, and tempted to take shortcuts. God wants us at peace. He has called us to peace. *He* is able to take care of everything we worry about, but no one can make the choice to fulfill the calling on our lives except us.

3. Read Luke 12:30-31. See? He will take care of everything we need; but there is a contingency to this promise. What is it? What is your primary concern right now? How is God specifically calling you to put His kingdom first?

4. Read Luke 12:32. Be nourished by the love in this verse. God loves to bless His children with gifts they could never earn or deserve. When we seek first His will in our lives, everything else will fall into place (see also Matthew 6:33). Is it easy for you to believe that He *loves* to give you good gifts? Explain.

5. Read Luke 12:33-34. Give whenever you can, love when it is not easy, and trust that God will take your offerings and multiply them to bless others and store up treasures in heaven for you. God's economy is beyond anything this world has to offer. In what ways do you feel inspired to give?

6. Read Luke 12:35-38. Take your time on these verses. Rid

your life of distractions and attitudes He is opposed to. He could come back any minute; be ready and burning with passion for Him. Write a personalized prayer out of these four verses. Ask the Lord to help you be alert and prepared for whatever He asks of you. Psalm 123:2 refers to a servant girl who keeps her eyes on her mistress, waiting for the slightest signal. Be *that* ready.

7. Read Luke 12:35-38 again. Look at it from the other side. Imagine you've lived a life of passion for the Lord. Try to picture the Lord of hosts putting on an apron and serving you. Imagine the feast prepared for those who love Him. Describe how this would make you feel.

8. Psalm 116:9 says, "And so I walk in the LORD's presence as I live here on earth!" Memorize this verse and walk every day in the light of His presence. Pause and pray. Ask God to inspire your walk of faith.

My precious sister, this is my prayer for you:

Dear friend, I am praying that all is well with you and that your body is as healthy as I know your soul is (3 John 1:2). So I have continued praying for you ever since I first heard about you. I ask God to give you a complete understanding of what he wants to do in your life and I ask him to make you wise with spiritual wisdom. Then the way you live will always honor and please the Lord, and you will continually do good, kind things for others. All the while, you will learn to know God better and better (adapted from Colossians 1:9-10).

Fifteen
What Words Do

May the words of my mouth and the thoughts of my heart be pleasing to you, O LORD, my rock and my redeemer.

PSALM 19:14

I USED TO BE A GOSSIP. I AM NOW IN MY FORTIES, and God has totally redeemed this area of my life, but many years ago I said things I shouldn't, I shared things that would have been better left unsaid, and I hashed things over with friends instead of bringing them straight to Jesus and trying to get the mind of Christ in the situation. On the one hand, I cringe when I think of the words that came out of me and never should have. On the other hand, I rejoice in the fact that not only has Christ forgiven me, He has literally turned my life around. I pray often for the people who hurt or bothered me back then, and for those I hurt.

Over the years as I grew up in the Lord, I more quickly sensed the Holy Spirit nudging me to close my lips and drop to my knees. I saw many things change and improve from my prayers where words would have only made a bad situation worse. Prayer changes a heart where judgment never could.

But it wasn't until something happened in my life, and *I* was on the receiving end of hateful gossip, that I realized something much more profound. As I lay on my floor in a heap of sobs brought about by words meant to injure me, I sensed Jesus kneeling on the floor at my side with His hand on my shoulder, saying, *I know how you feel. I've been there.* As I sat up and wiped my eyes, I came to understand a couple of things. First and foremost, the Lord showed me that our process, our journey, is *holy ground.* It is sacred to God. Our areas of struggle, insecurity, anger, and inconsistency mean something to Him, and He handles us with great care. It breaks His heart when we trample on someone else's holy ground with heavy steps, loud sighs, cutting words, and manipulative behavior. These actions are an affront to God and do nothing but injure people and give Christianity a bad name. "You realize, don't you, that you are the temple of God, and God himself is present in you? No one will get by with vandalizing God's temple, you can be sure of that. God's temple is sacred—and you, remember, are the temple" (1 Corinthians 3:16-17 MSG).

The other thing that became clear to me is this: When we women tear one another apart with our words, it isn't just a bad thing to do…it is treason. Imagine, if you will, a missionary ministering in a danger zone. Let's say in a moment of stress that she says something she shouldn't. Now imagine the following day that the offended woman is hiding in a back alley with a local government official who persecutes Christians. The missionary walks by and the offended one points her out and says, "There she is!" Wouldn't such a scenario shock you?

And yet every time we decide to be offended by another woman (that's right, we have a choice), and we begin to point out her flaws, her weak areas, and her deficits, the enemy is close by listening to every word we say. He is rubbing his hands together, glad to have one traitor on his side that will expose and speak curses (and not blessings) against the one who simply needs grace and forgiveness.

> Don't pick on people, jump on their failures, criticize their faults—unless, of course, you want the same treatment. That critical spirit has a way of boomeranging. It's easy to see a smudge on your neighbor's face and be oblivious to the ugly sneer on your own. Do you have the nerve to say, 'Let me wash your face for you,' when your own face is distorted by contempt? (Matthew 7:1-4 MSG).

Moving in the Right Direction

We have an aboveground pool in our backyard. Whenever we have a bunch of teens over, we do the "whirlpool." The teens jump in the water and get running in a circle along the outer edge of the pool. They create such a current that the water actually pulls down in the middle, creating a whirlpool. Then we count to three, and on three they all turn around and try to go the other way. The water smashes against them so hard it knocks most of them off their feet! Eventually, though, as they persist, the water moves in the other direction.

The thoughts we think and the words we say create a current all around us. We either invite the power of heaven in to influence our hearts and the world around us or we live defeated, scattered, petty lives in agreement with hell's desire for us. To change, we will at first encounter an unseen resistance, but if we persist, we will change the current in our lives. God wants us to be holy; Satan wants us to be catty. God wants us to be powerful; Satan wants us to be fearful. Choose this day whom you will serve.

Today I have given you the choice between life and
death, between blessings and curses. I call on heaven
and earth to witness the choice you make. Oh, that you
would choose life, that you and your descendants
might live! Choose to love the LORD your God and to
obey him and commit yourself to him, for he is your
life (Deuteronomy 30:19-20).

How shallow we can be when we allow small irritations to divide
us. We must become more pure in heart and strong in love. How
much grace do we have for others? How much forbearance? My
friend Sandy once said, "I never get too excited about a new friendship until we've had our first conflict; then I know what the friendship is made of."

Many of us have become too soft, too comfortable, and it takes
very little for us to take up an offense. Let's strive to be the kind of
true friend who would have to wade through more than an inch of
mud before we would turn back in disgust. We need to be able to
take a little more and still have much love to give. If this doesn't
apply to you, praise God. Use your strength to pray for women who
struggle in this area.

What does this have to do with balance? The Bible tells us that
our *own soul is nourished* when we are kind but that we *destroy ourselves* when we are cruel (Proverbs 11:17). Jesus said, "You are not
defiled by what you eat; *you are defiled by what you say and do*"
(Matthew 15:11, emphasis added).

Misspoken words have started wars, broken relationships, split
churches, crushed hopes, and wounded souls. The Bible says in
Proverbs 11:11 that "Through the blessing of the upright a city is
exalted, but by the mouth of the wicked it is destroyed" (NIV). A
whole city is destroyed by the words of someone's mouth! And yet it

is *through* "the blessings of the upright" that the world is affected for the better. In every sense of the word, we are to be "flow *through* accounts" for God to send His blessings to earth.

As we constantly seek the mind of Christ and His perspective, we will pray and speak from a heart that matches His. Henry Wadsworth Longfellow wrote, "Every man has his secret sorrows, which the world knows not; and often times we call a man cold when he is only sad." Before we judge, we must ask, "What must it be like for them?" "You must make allowance for each other's faults and forgive the person who offends you. Remember, the Lord forgave you, so you must forgive others" (Colossians 3:13).

Reasons Why We Gossip

Below are several reasons why women gossip. Take your time with this section. Search your heart and be encouraged. God's mercies are fresh and new every morning. Each day brings with it a chance to begin again.

Fear. "Fearing people is a dangerous trap, but to trust the Lord means safety" (Proverbs 29:25). We fight a losing battle when we seek to win the approval of all people all of the time. We live in community with imperfect people, and even the best of them sometimes have a wrong opinion or perspective. It's not just a trap; it's a dangerous trap to care too much about what others may be thinking about us. Do you want to be truly safe? Then walk in the fear of the Lord. As long as *you* don't gossip, as long as *you* don't judge, as long as *you* do what God tells you to do, then you will be safe. If you talk about others, you *will* get talked about. If you don't talk about others, you will still get talked about; but the difference is that you will be hidden in God and have *Him* as your defense. "Your goodness is so great! You have stored up great blessings for those who honor you.

You have done so much for those who come to you for protection, blessing them before the watching world. You hide them in the shelter of your presence, safe from those who conspire against them. You shelter them in your presence, far from accusing tongues" (Psalm 31:19-20).

Anger. "My dear brothers and sisters, be quick to listen, slow to speak, and slow to get angry. Your anger can never make things right in God's sight" (James 1:19-20). Anger is sometimes hurt that's been sitting a long time. As painful as it is, we must bring our disappointment and anger before the Lord. It's okay to cry, scream, yell, and beg God to make some sense of things. But then we need to forgive. When I wrestled through anger, it was like playing "hot potato." I'd toss my anger up to God, and within a few hours, I'd find it back in my lap again. I'd toss it up again, determined not to hang on to it, only to have it land in my lap again. But eventually, the "potato" stayed up for longer periods of time. As I prayed prayers of blessing on those who had hurt me deeply, my heart for them changed and eventually the potato disappeared. If there is unforgiveness in our hearts, nothing matters more than battling our way back to a place of love again. Unforgiveness poisons our soul and chases healthy relationships *and* the sense of God's presence far away from us. "Stop judging others, and you will not be judged. Stop criticizing others, or it will all come back on you. If you forgive others, you will be forgiven" (Luke 6:37).

No backbone. "Let your love, God, shape my life with salvation, exactly as you promised; then I'll be able to stand up to mockery because I trusted your Word" (Psalm 119:41-42 MSG). We always tell our kids regarding their choices in friends, "Don't hang around anyone you can't stand up to." It should be the same with us. If there is a friend who intimidates us and repeatedly drags us into conversations we don't want to be in, we either need to seek God for a fresh dose of courage or we need to consider spending less time with that person. "A gossip tells secrets, so don't hang around with someone who talks too much" (Proverbs 20:19).

Pride. "Pride comes before destruction, and an arrogant spirit before a fall" (Proverbs 16:18 HCSB). Truly, pride is just another form of insecurity. To be prideful means we've lost sight of who we are before the Lord, so we construct a bloated, lopsided picture of ourselves, emphasizing our good points and minimizing our bad ones. Pride is the most hideous of all sins. It's the very thing that got Satan kicked out of heaven. The moment we think we are something on our own, or that we are better than someone else, we position ourselves against the Almighty. I mentioned this verse earlier in the book but it bears repeating, "Though the LORD is great, he cares for the humble, but he keeps his distance from the proud" (Psalm 138:6). Nothing would break my heart more than to put myself up, put others down, and thereby cause the Lord to distance Himself from me. We all have moments where we slip into this kind of thinking, but we must keep a close watch on our hearts, our minds, and our words. Walk in a holy fear of the Lord. "You rescue those who are humble, but you humiliate the proud" (Psalm 18:27).

Envy. "You want what you don't have, so you scheme and kill to get it. You are jealous for what others have, and you can't possess it, so you fight and quarrel to take it away from them. And yet the reason you don't have what you want is that you don't ask God for it" (James 4:2). We have a good God. The reason we don't have what we want is that we haven't asked God for it. Or maybe we've asked Him but don't want to wait on His answer. Maybe someone else is enjoying a breakthrough or blessing we think we should have. We cannot hold on to envy and gratitude at the same time, so the best antidote for envy is thankfulness. When struggling with envy, we need to begin thanking God out loud for all the things we do have.

When we start naming our blessings, one by one, we'll notice all of the things we've been taking for granted. When we humble ourselves *and* our desires before the Almighty God, and leave them there, in due time we will see movement and breakthrough in our lives. Envy kills our joy. The joy of the Lord is our strength. We must rid our lives of any hint of envy. "So clean house! Make a clean sweep of malice and pretense, envy and hurtful talk. You've had a taste of God. Now, like infants at the breast, drink deep of God's pure kindness. Then you'll grow up mature and whole in God" (1 Peter 2:1-3 MSG). "A heart at peace gives life to the body, but envy rots the bones" (Proverbs 14:30 NIV).

Boredom. "No, we neither make nor save ourselves. God does both the making and saving. He creates each of us by Christ Jesus to join him in the work he does, the good work he has gotten ready for us to do, *work we had better be doing*" (Ephesians 2:10 MSG, emphasis added). Women who are bored and unfulfilled tend to struggle most with gossip. When our lives have no vision or passion, it is all too easy to find fault with those who do. Women who have a sense of direction and vision *do* have faults like anybody else, but at least they are going somewhere and doing something with their lives. If we're really concerned about them, we can pray for them. Otherwise, we need to put that watchful eye on ourselves and allow God to call us higher and grant us a vision for the specific calling on our life. We are made for so much more than we can imagine. "We who believe are carefully joined together, becoming a holy temple for the Lord" (Ephesians 2:21).

Here is the critical point: We do damage to one another when we speak from an impure, mixed-motive heart. We must not misrepresent God with our words. God is love, and in Him there is no darkness at all. So when our heart is darkened with bitterness, judgment, and a critical spirit, we need to close our lips, humble ourselves, and ask the Lord to renew our heart. This is not a small deal…this is a very big deal. Our tongue can destroy a city, a church, or someone's life (along with our own). For out of the heart the mouth speaks. "A good person produces good deeds from a good heart, and an evil person produces evil deeds from an evil heart. *Whatever is in your heart determines what you say*" (Luke 6:45, emphasis added).

I love these words from A.W. Tozer:

> The heart's fierce effort to protect itself from every slight, to shield its touchy honor from the bad opinion of friend and enemy, will never let the mind have rest. Continue this fight through the years and the burden will become intolerable. Yet the sons of earth are carrying this burden continually, challenging every word spoken against them, cringing under every criticism, smarting under each fancied slight, tossing sleepless if another is preferred before them. Such a burden is not necessary to bear. Jesus calls us to His rest, and meekness is His method. The meek man cares not at all who is greater than he, for he has long ago decided that the esteem of the world is not worth the effort. He develops toward himself a kindly sense of humor and learns to say, "Oh, so you have been overlooked? They have placed someone else before you? They have whispered that you are pretty small stuff after all? And now you feel hurt because the world is saying about you the very things you have been saying about yourself? Only yesterday you were telling God that you were nothing, a mere worm of the dust. Where is your consistency? Come on, humble yourself and cease to care what men think."[1]

It's time to raise the standard! The verses below are ones I have either memorized or am currently working on; maybe they will help you:

> Hear me, you who know what is right, you people who have my law in your hearts; do not fear the reproach of men or be terrified by their insults (Isaiah 51:7 NIV).

> The LORD is my light and my salvation, whom shall I fear? The LORD is the stronghold of my life, of whom shall I be afraid? (Psalm 27:1 NIV).

> A wise man's heart guides his mouth, and his lips promote instruction (Proverbs 16:23 NIV).

> Take control of what I say, O LORD, and keep my lips sealed (Psalm 141:3).

> I have hidden your word in my heart, that I might not sin against you (Psalm 119:11).

> A wise woman builds her house; a foolish woman tears hers down with her own hands (Proverbs 14:1).

> An unreliable messenger stumbles into trouble, but a reliable messenger brings healing (Proverbs 13:17).

> In quietness and confidence will be your strength (Isaiah 30:15, my paraphrase).

> If you keep your mouth shut, you'll stay out of trouble (Proverbs 21:23).

> I will open my mouth with skillful and godly wisdom and in my tongue will be the law of kindness (Proverbs 31:26, my paraphrase).

> The words of the godly save lives (Proverbs 12:6).

These next two verses fill me with such a sense of awareness of how much our words mean to God that they make me want to submit my every thought to Him before I speak it out.

> I have put my words in your mouth and covered you with the shadow of my hand (Isaiah 51:16 NIV).

> [He] carries out the words of his servants and fulfills the predictions of his messengers (Isaiah 44:26 NIV).

If we want our words to be a wellspring of life, we must stay close to the well. Our words will nourish and build up when our focus shifts from what others are doing *to us* to what God has done *for us*. And He has been good.

Lord of heaven,

Purify my heart! Grant me a new perspective and a greater desire to please You. You are all I need. Help me not to get stuck in wounds and hurts from my past. Life is too precious to throw it away like that. Please, Lord, bless every person I have ever hurt with my words, and help me to bless every person who has ever hurt me. It's not enough to speak kind words if my heart is fuming. I want a change from the inside out. Heal the deepest parts of me, restore my joy, and make me whole again. Redeem my past, refresh my relationship with You, and renew my resolve to love others. I need You every single hour. I am glad You're right here with me now. I love You. Amen.

Steps Toward Health

- If there are any offenses hanging over my head, I will pause right now, ask forgiveness where I need to, bless those who have hurt me, and accept God's mercy for my past.

- If I struggle with a critical spirit, I will get alone with God and ask Him why. I will continually bring this struggle before the Lord until I am free of it.

- I will regularly check my heart for bad attitudes, judgments, and criticism. As soon as I notice, I will bring these things before God. I am determined to keep my heart free and clear of anything that will choke out the fresh life I have in Christ.

- I will begin to speak blessings out loud. I will bless my family, my church, my neighborhood, and my enemies. I will even bless myself.

- I will sing more often.

- I will memorize Scripture. I will hide it in my heart and allow it to be the standard for my soul.

- Even when I blow it, I will not let the knowledge of God's love get away from me.

TRY THIS

- When you're in a group and gossip starts up, confront the situation, redirect the conversation, or walk away. Just don't expose yourself to that kind of garbage. "When you run out of wood, the fire goes out; when the gossip ends, the quarrel dies down" (Proverbs 26:20 MSG).

- Ask God to protect you during weak and vulnerable moments when you are apt to say something you shouldn't. "Free me from hidden traps; I want to hide in you" (Psalm 31:4 MSG).

- Never trust *anyone* with words that shouldn't be said.

- Talk less and listen more. "Everyone must be quick to hear, slow to speak" (James 1:19 HCSB).

- Read Scripture out loud on a regular basis. It will change your life. "For the word of God is full of living power. It is sharper than the sharpest knife, cutting deep into our innermost thoughts and desires. It exposes us for what we really are" (Hebrews 4:12).

- Purify your self-talk. Pay attention to the things you tell yourself, and line up your words with the promises in Scripture.

- Instead of negative, binding phrases such as "This will never work out" or "Things always go this way for me," make bold proclamations of God's goodness such as "Thanks be to God, who always leads me in His triumph!" and "I am so thankful to be a child of God and know that nothing is impossible with Him!" Take hold of all that's been taken hold of for you.

- Use the eight gatekeepers from chapter 12 as standards for your words. Remember them? We are to fix our thoughts on whatever is true, honorable, right, pure, lovely, admirable, excellent, and worthy of praise. One qualifier here: If something is true, but there is no love in your heart, close your mouth and trust the Lord to bring someone along whose heart is in the right place. "The whole point of what we're urging is simply love—love uncontaminated by self-interest and counterfeit faith, a life open to God. Those who fail to keep to this point soon wander off into cul-de-sacs of gossip" (1 Timothy 1:5-6 MSG).

Balance Application

God has deposited a lot of good in us. Think of the countless church services you've been allowed to attend without fear for your life. Think of the people He has put in your life just to love you. Think of the beautiful sunny days He has allowed you to enjoy. Think of the sunsets that have taken your breath away. In ways too numerous to count, He has given good things to you and to me. We must not allow the precious truth of His love to get lost in translation. The world needs to see and hear and experience what He is giving. If we hold on to useless weights, past mistakes, and old wounds, people will receive an inconsistent message of God's grace. Our lives are the message that Christ's love heals every hurt, delivers every promise, and forgives every sin. Look at the following verse not only as someone who delivers a message, but as someone who is the message: "An unreliable messenger stumbles into trouble, but a reliable messenger brings healing" (Proverbs 13:17). Can you think of a greater honor than being a humble, reliable messenger of God's grace and love?

Study Time

We're going to do something a little different for this study time. We are going to take a look at a passage from Isaiah, using the Message paraphrase. I think you'll enjoy it.

1. Read Isaiah 58:7: "What I'm interested in seeing you do is: sharing your food with the hungry, inviting the homeless poor into your homes, putting clothes on the shivering ill-clad, being available to your own families." This

verse truly expresses Christ's heart for those in need. Pause, pray, and ask the Lord to show you what you can do for those in need. Ask Him to speak to you about your availability to your own family. Write down what He speaks to you. Determine to *do* what He tells you to.

2. Read Isaiah 58:8-9: "Do this and the lights will turn on, and your lives will turn around at once. Your righteousness will pave your way. The GOD of glory will secure your passage. Then when you pray, GOD will answer. You'll call out for help and I'll say, 'Here I am.'" Look at and list the seven things that will happen in your life if you "do this." Don't just go through the motions. Pause and think about how your life would be affected for the better if you were doing what God is "interested in seeing you do" (verse 7).

3. Read Isaiah 58:9: "If you get rid of unfair practices, quit blaming victims, quit gossiping about other people's sins..." Make yourself think about times you've been unfair, summed up someone else's suffering, and gossiped about someone else's sins. If you've not repented over these actions, do so now. Otherwise, pause and pray that God would heighten your conviction in these areas. Ask Him to make you more holy, just, and compassionate. Write out a prayer.

4. Read Isaiah 58:10: "If you are generous with the hungry and start giving yourselves to the down-and-out..." Write down the most recent thing you've done for the hungry. Write down a way you've helped someone who was down-and-out. Take a moment and lift those offerings up to God. Imagine the smile on His face. Ask Him to multiply your gift in the lives of those you blessed.

Ask God to make you more aware of the needs around you, and then meet those needs as best you can.

5. Read Isaiah 58:10: "Your lives will begin to glow in the darkness, your shadowed lives will be bathed in sunlight." We live in a dark world, and yet you will *glow* in the darkness and *feel* the warmth of the sunlight on the darkest days when you care for the "least of these" (see Matthew 25:40), just as Jesus did. Write a personalized prayer asking God to give you a Christlike heart for the lowly in this world.

6. Read Isaiah 58:11: "I will always show you where to go. I'll give you a full life in the emptiest of places—firm muscles, strong bones. You'll be like a well-watered garden, a gurgling spring that never runs dry." This is a picture of a strong, healthy life inside and out. This verse speaks of fresh life springing forth; of being a "flow-through account" for the power of God. Rewrite this verse in a personalized prayer.

7. Read Isaiah 58:12: "You'll use the old rubble of past lives to build anew, rebuild the foundations from out of your past. You'll be known as those who can fix anything, restore old ruins, rebuild and renovate, make the community livable again." If you keep your heart pure and stay close to God, you will be used as a master builder, a healer. You will be known as someone who can fix and restore and renovate lives. You will have clean hands, a pure heart, and speak words that heal. Make this your highest aim. Write down a prayer of faith, asking God for everything He wants to give you and everything He wants to make of you.

Sixteen

A Deeper Rest

*God's promise of entering his place of rest
still stands, so we ought to tremble with fear
that some of you might fail to get there.*

HEBREWS 4:1

I HAVE A FEELING THAT THIS IS GOING TO BE A tough chapter for me to write. As I sit here with my face in my hands, waiting on the Lord, asking Him to show me where to start, I sense that He wants me to give you an inside look at a time in my life that I would rather forget. In fact, I think I hear the phone ringing now...I'll be right back. Okay, I am stalling. I'll get to the point. I am going to let you in on a time when I was so severely out of balance that I'm pretty sure I was on the verge of a breakdown.

As I mentioned earlier in the book, I have been speaking at retreats and conferences for a number of years. Since the day of that phone call from my long-lost friend, I've known that my calling is to speak and write to women. God graciously and wisely kept my ministry opportunities in pace with the stages of my boys' lives and my family's needs. I clearly saw this as His provision and protection on my life. Still, I looked forward to that day when I would be able to put more time into my writing.

It finally looked as though that season of life had come for me a number of years ago. My boys were all in school full days, and whatever time I wasn't putting into speaking preparations I was ready to put into writing. I knew with all my heart this was something God had called me to. I looked forward to every chance I had to sit down and write. I had met a number of important people in the literary world, and it seemed as though God was preparing me to take hold of my dream.

One morning my husband and I received a call from our pastor. We'd been attending a little church for about a year. We love our pastor and his wife. They are some of the most humble, God-fearing people we have ever met. We were delighted at the chance to meet them for breakfast. So there we sat, in a booth at the restaurant. After some small talk, our pastor got right to the point. He leaned in and asked, "Would you two prayerfully consider running our youth program?"

I sat back in the booth somewhat surprised by the question. Kevin and I had worked with youth in the past. We absolutely love teenagers. We also knew what running a program entailed: time, time, and more time. Kevin and I looked at each other, and then he replied, "Well, we will definitely pray about it." I was sure they had the wrong people. There was nothing in my heart that wanted to take on a whole youth program.

God had confirmed His call on my life many times and in many ways. I saw Him do amazing things in the hearts of women at many of my engagements. The primary burden in my heart was to minister to women. If we took this volunteer position to oversee and run the youth program, would I be able to still book speaking engagements? And when would I write? I had waited so long to be in a season of life that allowed me time to pursue what God had put on my heart. I loved the idea of opening our home to teens, but to run the program? Surely this couldn't be God's plan for me!

But as I bowed my head and prayed…as I asked God to show me His will… I was surprised to sense that God was indeed calling us to do this. I didn't want to. This call from God completely crossed my will. But I feared God enough to know that if I ran away from obedience I would just be running into the desert (or be swallowed by a whale). I had been a Christian long enough to know that one way to kill your intimacy with the Lord is to be slow to obey, partially obey, or to not obey at all.

We poured our hearts and souls into this youth group. And I came to know the teens and absolutely fell in love with them. We worked hard and God stretched us. We saw God move in the hearts of these kids over and over again. This ministry allowed us to have our kids with us all of the time. Many events were held in our home, and the boys were right in the center of it all. We grew in numbers and in strength.

After a year of youth ministry, I was asked to join the leadership of our church. It was a great honor to be asked, and after praying about it, both Kevin and I agreed that I should serve in this capacity. I am embarrassed to tell you, though, that eventually I also joined the worship team, I occasionally served as the service leader (the person who opens the service with the welcome and announcements), and I gave the Sunday sermon once in a while. I was also teaching aerobics part-time. And at the same time, in addition to his regular job, my husband was heading up the church's building program, which entailed about 20 hours a week for more than a year.

Even with all these ministry opportunities, I was still speaking, still a mom, still a wife, and still faced a mountain of dishes and laundry every single week. I had slowly, gradually, one choice at a time, spread myself so thin that I thought I would snap. This put a strain on relationships, my perspective became skewed, my energy level was as low as it was when I was sick, and the sense of God's presence in my life came and went. I was desperate for relief, but it seemed far out of my reach.

What in the world possessed me to get involved in so many things? There are probably a number of answers to that question, but the primary one is this: I wanted to help out. I realized that God was postponing my dream of writing and, therefore, I had determined this to be the season where we were to work hard to fill in the gaps at our little church. I knew without a doubt that we were called there to serve. I also knew that if I had disobeyed God and tried to prematurely pursue my dream (like writing eight hours a day trying to achieve it), God would not have blessed my efforts. I had to lay down my dream and pick up my cross. Still, God's yoke fits perfectly, and yet I was nearly crushed beneath my load. So where did I go wrong?

I once spoke to a man who was unfaithful to his spouse, and when asked how he could do such a thing, he had a most profound answer. He said, "I kept changing the rules, a little at a time." I'll never forget those words. I think that's what happened with me. I figured that because I was called to serve, I would throw myself into the task. I had the best of intentions and saw a measure of fruit coming from the things I was doing. So little by little I added more commitments to my life, and every other area of my life was forced to accommodate what I was giving out. As a result, I experienced weakness in areas where I once was strong. I spent far too much time on "output" and far too little time being nourished and resting. I gave away all of my time, and with it all of my peace.

One day I went over to my neighbor's house. I was troubled and stressed and needed someone to pray with me. As I sat at her table and described how I was feeling, she responded quickly by saying,

"I know a speaker who teaches on this very thing!" I grabbed a pen and a piece of paper, leaned in, and said, "Give me her name!" She poked me in the forehead and said, "*You*, you goofball." What a wake-up call. Years ago God had given me profound concepts to share on health and balance, and I wasn't applying any of them. Things had to change.

Balance Is Just the Beginning

One night I met a friend for dinner. I brought with me a list of every role I was filling. We put that list on the table, put our hands over it, and prayed, "Lord God, please give wisdom and clarity tonight. Show us which commitments You are blessing and which ones You are not. Amen." We discussed each commitment in depth until I could see for myself which things I was doing out of obligation or for fun or because I lacked the faith that God would care for me.

One by one, as the Lord led me, I cut every extra commitment from my life with the exception of the couple things God was still blessing and anointing me to do. Since it took me many months of running at that frantic pace to see (and feel) the insanity in it all, it took some time to restore my life to a place of balance, peace, and rest.

Oh, how we miss the wonder of who God is when we run the rat race! Learning the basics of godly, balanced living *is just the very beginning*. Once we learn to appropriate biblical truths that make our lives more fruitful and run more smoothly, we've only laid a foundation for the greater work to begin.

As we slow down and understand why we don't have to be running in a dozen directions, when we find in our souls the inner security that proclaims, "I have nothing to prove and everything to gain by keeping the main things the main things!" then we are able to see, to hear, and to be a part of the divinely creative and powerful things God is doing.

When we are scattered and depleted, we are barely able to pray. When we slow down a bit (but not enough), we pray, but all too often the prayers are one-sided. We unload all of our stresses at the feet of Jesus and then we zip to our next appointment. Now, Jesus is gracious and merciful. He loves us so much that He will move in whatever context we allow Him to. But still, He has so much to say to us, so much to show us, so much to teach us.

Far more than having a place to go with all of our stresses, Jesus' heart is a place we can live from, draw from, and learn from. As we bring balance to our lives in a way that allows us room to grow, room to listen, and room to respond, we will see the blessedness of living a life with room to breathe. If we want to maintain balance, and if we truly want to grow, we must give God room to work in our lives.

I am so very thankful that the Lord allowed me to exhaust myself the way I did. I learned a life lesson I will never forget. I will never again allow myself to take on more than God is anointing me for. I understand now more than ever that in the long run, when I do too much, I am not really helping in the best way possible. I am hurting myself, my health, and my relationships.

Overcommitment kills relationships and steals our joy. A profound lesson in walking out our faith and serving as God leads is *doing more* doesn't necessarily *produce more*. Walking closely with the Lord and doing what He says, does. In John 15:5, Jesus said that we bear *much* fruit by staying close to Him (not by doing more; by abiding more).

We are called to live lives of peace and power (God's peace and God's power). In our lives, power is diminished—not enhanced—when we do more than we are called to. Joy increases and fruit is plentiful when we do things with the strength that God provides. When our lives have room to breathe, the wonder of all God has for us returns like a breath of fresh air. God loves us. He wants us to be full of joy and peace. He knows that *when* we are full of these things, *then* we will serve Him out of that fullness. "When you come to him, that fullness comes together for you, too. His power extends over everything. Entering into this fullness is not something you figure out or achieve" (Colossians 2:10-11 MSG).

A number of years have passed since my time of total depletion. Now I enjoy hours in His presence and an increased capacity to understand His Word and His ways, and I have an overwhelming sense of what I am to put my hand to each new day. More power and focus have emerged from my life than I could ever have imagined. There is nothing like intimacy with God. *Nothing* matters more than our oneness with Him. When we make time for Him, we understand our need for Him, and then we hunger for more of Him.

If you are too busy to slow down and be filled, you are too busy. No matter what season of life you are in, God has made you for Himself and therefore provides a way to fill you with Himself. We all have work to do. And the more we have going on, the more we need His input in our lives.

That Place of Rest

Why *not* embrace a peaceful life if it's been provided for us? What is keeping us from swimming upstream if we have to, to get to a place of perpetual peace and rest? Through my own experience I learned that spiritual rest isn't a luxury or simply a benefit of being a Christian; it is a mandate from our holy and powerful God. We are warned in Hebrews that if we don't enter the rest God has for us, we will fall. "So there is a special rest still waiting for the people of God.

For all who enter into God's rest will find rest from their labors, just as God rested after creating the world. Let us do our best to enter that place of rest. For anyone who disobeys God, as the people of Israel did, will fall" (Hebrews 4:9-11).

Why do we make sure our kids get to bed at a decent time night after night? It is because if they wear down, they will melt down. They will get sick, lose perspective, and will not be able to function to their fullest. It's the same with us. God is our Father, and He knows that if we don't rest, we will fall. We will fall into bad habits, shortcuts, temptations, and sickness. We will fall out of earshot of His voice and miss the wisdom our day requires. Instead of gaining more ground and pursuing *increased* health and fruitfulness, we will *lose* ground and with it our peace, our strength, and our effectiveness.

In previous chapters we touched lightly on Sabbath moments and Sabbath days. Now we'll look at two more aspects of rest. What I want to accomplish in this chapter is a whole shift in perspective. We *must* get out of the rat race. We must resist the frantic, harried lifestyle that our culture has come to embrace. It's not good for our health, our families, or the health of the church. What God supplies is far better.

Sabbath seasons. There may be seasons in your life where you are led by God *not* to be involved in any defined ministry *for the purpose of* healing, training, refining, rest, and seeking a deeper relationship with Him. During such times you will spend extended hours in quiet, in study, and prayer. For a time you will pull back from much of your outward activity so more energy can go into strengthening and deepening your spiritual roots. Of course, this doesn't mean you rest from serving the Lord. You can still go to church or to the grocery store or walk through your neighborhood and find someone who needs a blessing. As a child of God, you will always have the high privilege of being at His service. "All must give as they are able, according to the blessings given to them by the LORD your God" (Deuteronomy 16:17).

A Sabbath heart. "Those who live in the shelter of the Most High will find rest in the shadow of the Almighty. This I declare of the LORD: He alone is my refuge, my place of safety; he is my God, and I am trusting him" (Psalm 91:1-2). This psalm says it better than I ever could. Look at the first part of this verse. When we set up camp under the protection of the Most High God, we will be able to rest there. When we *live* closely with the Lord, we can *rest* in His *shadow.* Imagine Him hovering over, protecting all who come to Him for refuge. When we quit trying to control everything and everybody in our lives, and instead entrust our cares to God, He will lift them from our shoulders. When storm clouds press in, circumstances heat up, or people ask for too much, we will not allow these things to lure us out of His shadow. Instead, we will stay in that hidden place of rest and trust and pray, "Lord, I see these things coming at me, threatening to disrupt the peace that I have in You. Would You hold these things for me? Would You hand them to me one at a time and grant me Your wisdom and perspective? I want to stay hidden with You. I know You are strong and powerful, so I will refuse to worry or be anxious. I will look to You to carry the world on Your shoulders while I rest and trust in Your glorious strength. I, like the psalmist, am trusting You." This doesn't mean you won't have to rise to the challenge of difficult circumstances or demanding people, but you can do so with a heart that refuses to enter into the stressful intensity of the age. God has called us to peace. "For he will rescue you from every trap and protect you from the fatal plague. He will shield you with his wings. He will shelter you with his feathers. His faithful promises are your armor and protection" (Psalm 91:3-4). We have every reason to trust in Him. The lie of the age is that God is not for us. Satan works tirelessly to steal our assurance and our peace. We have to fight for it. And, sister, this is a battle worth fighting.

Father God,

I couldn't ask You to give more than You already have. I am overwhelmed by the gift of Your Son. Every morning I wake up to fresh mercies, fresh nourishment, and fresh power from above. Help me to find that sacred place of rest in You; and when I find it, help me to set up camp there. Help me to live there. I long to please You with my faith; a faith that declares, "My God is for me, who can stand against me?" There is so much more You want to pour into me. Help me, Lord, to slow down long enough to receive it. Oh, how I love You. Increase my hunger and desire for Your presence. You are everything to me. Amen.

Steps Toward Health

- I will make it a point to slow down this week. I will cut something out of my schedule if I have to. I will use that time to sit in God's presence.

- I will get up a little earlier in the morning to spend time with God. I will "ask nicely" by getting up ten minutes earlier each day this week so my body can get used to the change. I will remember that *any* time I set aside for God will eventually produce supernatural results.

- I will daily (hourly, if necessary), hand over my worries and cares to the Lord. I will diligently seek the peace He provides.

- I will put "a restful, peaceful heart" at the top of my prayer list for myself, my loved ones, and even for my enemies.

- I will memorize Scripture relating to rest and peace. I will use this as my weapon against the threats and harassments of the devil. (Here are a few to help you get started.)

  - "My soul finds rest in God alone, my salvation comes from him" (Psalm 62:1 NIV). Two things stand out to me with this verse. My soul is to find rest in God alone. Not when all my relationships are running smoothly, when my checkbook balances perfectly, or when it seems that everybody likes me at the moment. No, I only find my rest in the *fact* that God is enough for me in spite of everything else. The other thing that stands out is this: If I can trust Him for my salvation, surely I can trust Him with every lesser thing.

  - "Be at rest once more, O my soul, for the LORD has been good to you" (Psalm 116:7 NIV). If we've been lured out of our rest, we simply need to recall once again all the ways God has been faithful. Then we proclaim, "And my God will be faithful again."

  - "Let the peace of Christ rule in your hearts, since as members of one body you were called to peace. And be thankful" (Colossians 3:15 NIV). What strikes me with this verse is the word "let." God is daily pouring Himself out to us; we just need to let it in. As we open ourselves up to His influence and perspective, His peace will rule our hearts because we will look at life with God in mind. This point also bears repeating: Never let go of thankfulness.

TRY THIS

* Spend a portion of your quiet time in total silence. Fix your thoughts solely on God and His ability to speak the mountains into existence and to stir up the waters by the very sound of His voice. Allow yourself to be assured that the One you are coming to is strong and mighty. At first you may struggle with wandering thoughts; stick with it. It takes practice, but the payoff is priceless. Silence before the Lord opens a doorway to immeasurable peace and understanding. Read these wonderful verses: Isaiah 30:18, 40:31, and 64:4.

* Write down some of the things the Lord speaks to you during this time. Reflect on them the following day. Sometimes you will gain more clarity a day later.

* Examine your heart throughout the day. As soon as you notice a lack of peace or increased anxiety, retrace your steps until you find which thought or circumstance disrupted your peace. Often those instances are symptomatic of some deeper issues God wants to get at in our lives. He wants to deliver us of anything that the enemy can use against us.

* Let your children see you committing yourself daily to the Lord. Pray with them before meals, before they go to school, before a doctor appointment, or after you've had the privilege of purchasing groceries. Let it be commonplace to thank God for a good report from the doctor, for food in the cupboard, or for protection on the road. Allow them to see you bringing God into every avenue of your life.

* Be careful with your "anxious confessions." If your children hear you worrying out loud, they will pick up on it. More

often than not, allow them to hear statements of faith coming from your mouth.

* Daily confess, "Lord, You are strong and You love me. I will trust in You today."

Balance Application

It really is a matter of belief. Will God come through for me if I put more on His shoulders than I put on my own? There is a certain feeling that if we don't worry about everything, we'll get lackadaisical and everything will fall apart. On the contrary, the kind of rest we are called to has a focus and purpose to it. When we are living in the shelter of the Most High, we will have a front row seat to see with our spiritual eyes and hear with our spiritual ears what God is doing in the world, in the hearts of our loved ones, and in our own lives. We are far more effective living close to the Source with a heart of rest than we are running in a thousand directions amid the clamor of the world. We are representatives of the Most High God and yet still fully human. We need our physical rest, we need occasional extended bouts of spiritual rest, and we need to live from a heart that fully trusts and fully rests in its Almighty Father.

Study Time

1. Read Psalm 84:1-2. Read it again, but this time read aloud with a heart of passion.

2. How uncomfortable was that for you? Mark this spot in

your Bible and come back to it again and again, reading this passage out loud until your passionate words match the cry of your heart.

3. Read Psalm 84:3-4. Think for a moment how all of nature recognizes the Lord. Life flows from Him and finds its place of rest in His presence. Why are those who dwell in God's presence blessed (happy)? Write down some of your thoughts.

4. Read Psalm 84:5-7. We will pass through valleys and storms. But more important than our circumstances is that we are headed somewhere. We are on a pilgrimage, heading toward a promise. And as we venture out, determined to follow our Lord when it is popular and when it isn't, we will find strength and pools of blessing where there were none. What have been the highs and lows of your journey? Write them down. Remember, you are strong in the Lord.

5. Read Psalm 84:8-10. Notice the persistence and passion in this prayer. Sometimes we need to press in until we get a breakthrough. The psalmist was after something here. He was determined to find his hidden place with the Lord because he knew what was waiting for him. Have you experienced such sweetness in God's presence where you can honestly say, "Better is one day in Your courts than a thousand elsewhere"? If your answer is yes, than allow that to encourage you to live even closer to your Source. If your answer is no, you are in for a treat. Wherever you are, write down a prayer for increased passion for the presence of God.

6. Read Psalm 84:11. There are countless treasures available for those who walk closely with the Lord. Write down the five things listed in this verse but leave a little space. Now expound on each of the five. How do these blessings affect you personally?

7. Read Psalm 84:12. Why does blessing come to the one who trusts in the Lord? Explain it the best you can.

8. Read Psalm 62:5-6. Write out these verses in a personalized prayer of faith.

Seventeen
A Focused Life

The gatekeeper opens the gate to him and the sheep recognize his voice. He calls his own sheep by name and leads them out. When he gets them all out, he leads them and they follow because they are familiar with his voice.

JOHN 10:3-4 MSG

SHE WOULD LIKE TO SEE YOU NOW," BOB SAID softly on the phone. I looked up at Kevin, who nodded toward the door. We drove in silence. Kevin would speed up in effort to get to her quickly, and then slow down as if to put off for a bit what we were about to see.

We entered the house and went up the stairs to the living room. All of Peggy's knickknacks had been gathering dust. Dishes were in the sink and the cookie jar was empty. In the middle of the living room was her hospital bed. Her frail body lay motionless under the sheet. Her head was turned to the side, and I could see that her eyes were partially opened. Saliva ran from the side of her mouth as she labored to breathe.

I forced back the lump in my throat as I moved closer. I gently reached over the bed railing to touch her arm. Her skin tore like a wet napkin. I quickly looked up at the nurse and gasped. "I'm so sorry!" The nurse reassured me with "Peggy cannot feel much of anything right now, but it would be best if you would just touch her fingers and look into her eyes when you speak to her."

My mentor was dying. She had throat cancer, which had spread to other parts of her body. I was sick at the same time with Lyme disease. She had often ministered to me as if I were sicker than she was. When I couldn't handle it anymore and would cry out to God on her behalf, she would touch my hand to quiet me. Peggy would then say, "My Lord will take me when He gets more glory from my death than He does from my life."

Beautiful, lovely Peggy was preparing to meet Jesus. I would miss her terribly. "I love you, Peggy, and I always will." I sucked in a sob and continued, "You have taught me many things…I want to be just like you…Jesus is getting your place all ready for you. I love you so much." I wept as her eyes pierced my soul and her body lay perfectly still. When Kevin stepped in front of her gaze, she moved her head slightly and mouthed two words to him. We all stepped in to hear what was important enough for her to spend such precious energy.

She curled her fingertips around his hand and opened her eyes a little wider. Again she mouthed the words, "Love her." Peggy knew that I was weak and would need Kevin's strength in the days ahead. Both of my hands covered my mouth and tears came like a flood. I needed to wail. Kevin wrapped his hands around her frail fingers and said, "I promise, Peggy. I will forever." That was the last time I saw my mentor and friend Peggy Pearson.

Peggy was a woman after God's own heart. I believe that God did not want to go another minute without her by His side. She was more like Jesus than even her husband, Bob, knew…and he loved her immensely. A flood of people came to the funeral and squeezed into the sanctuary. Bob didn't know many of these people, and yet they came. They came to pay tribute to a woman who had blessed them. She gave gifts to complete strangers but told no one, not even Bob.

"I met Peggy on a bus and didn't have money for lunch. Peggy fed me." "I met Peggy at the hospital, and she bought me a cup of coffee and listened to my story." "Peggy brought me many meals when my husband lost his job." One by one people got in line to share their story of how Peggy touched their lives and pointed them to Jesus.

Bob stood there with tears streaming down his face as he learned that his wife was even lovelier than he knew.

Peggy lived the abiding life. In other words, she stayed close to her Father's heart. She embraced the truth that Christ was the source of all she would ever need. Through every season of her life—in her waiting and in her suffering—she never doubted the *goodness* of God. Peggy was a spiritual giant, though to the world she looked like a frail, aging woman. In the Psalms we are told that God is not impressed with our strength or success; those things are puny in His sight. But what He delights in, what makes His heart beat faster, is someone who honors Him and continually trusts in His *unfailing love;* especially when the storms come (Psalm 147:10-11). Trusting is sometimes costly, but anything worth pursuing always is. Jesus told us that the water He gives would allow us to never thirst again. His water is pure and fresh and new (John 4:14). Yet we continue to dig our own wells and drink muddy water because sometimes it just seems easier (Jeremiah 2:13).

Peggy believed that this world was not her home, and she lived like someone just passing through. She hung all of her hopes and dreams on heaven's door and knew they were safe there. Her value, identity, and motivation were fueled by a love that surpassed anything the earth had to offer. Peggy held much of what she owned with an open hand because she understood the limitations of her earthly treasures. But she clung tightly to her precious Savior, knowing her kingdom investment was a sound one.

I pray that we can live the way Peggy did. When we are lonely, let us wait for the one God is preparing for us. When we are hurting, may our medication be the healing balm of His precious blood. When we are angry with someone, may our retaliation be a fierce prayer of blessing on their behalf. When we are excited, may we not get ahead of God, but rather take our every cue from Him. This is the living, breathing fellowship of the abiding life. Instead of digging our little makeshift wells, let us stay close to the living water of Christ and trust Him with all that we need. May we determine not to live on fast food when He has prepared a feast for us. Lord, help us to stay close to You!

What Is Your Focal Point?

When I was a young gymnast, I learned the main component of balance: focus. I could walk swiftly and leap on a balance beam. I could do cartwheels and back walkovers and turns as long as I focused on one single point. As I fixed my eyes on the end of the beam, I could make difficult things look easy, I could walk straight without bobbling, and I could get off the beam in one piece.

As we fix our eyes heavenward on Jesus, we will live in a way that makes difficult things look easy, we will run and not stumble, and we will get there in one piece. We have many things to worry about, but there's only one thing to truly concern ourselves with, and that's keeping our hearts set on the Lord Jesus.

In Luke 10, Mary and Martha welcomed Jesus into their home. Both wanted to be near Him, both wanted to serve Him. Martha hurried to and fro, stressing about the *food* when the *Source* of all life was sitting in her living room. Mary, on the other hand, sat at Jesus' feet and soaked in everything He had to say. Martha complained to Jesus and asked Him to talk to Mary. And this was His reply: "But the Lord said to her, 'My dear Martha, you are so upset over all these details! There is really only one thing worth being concerned about. Mary has discovered it—and I won't take it away from her'" (Luke 10:41-42).

There is really only *one thing* worth being concerned about. Jesus said this knowing that the pace of life would spin out of control. Especially for this reason, He has called us to His side. Mary wasn't scolded for not helping; she was praised for keeping her eyes on Him. Living an abiding life means we sometimes let go of certain things so we can do the *one thing*. I've noticed in my own life that when I leave undone the lesser for the sake of the greater, God multiplies my time and I usually get the lesser done also. And I did so without forsaking the most important thing. In the Psalms, David also understood the call: "The one thing I ask of the LORD—the thing I seek most—is to live in the house of the LORD all the days of my life, delighting in the LORD's perfections and meditating in his Temple" (Psalm 27:4).

Dear sister, this is at the very core of a healthy life and a heart at rest...a life *focused* on the Lord, a life *absorbed* with the love that pours out of heaven daily, a life *fully committed* to doing what God asks. A life such as this will go from strength to strength and shine ever brighter until the full light of day (Proverbs 4:18). This is the life of spiritual balance: a life that centers on and draws from heaven's love. This love is never stagnant. It is always growing, always refining, and always dealing with sin and healing pain. It is always flowing in, making a difference, and then flowing out to a lost and dying world. Take Him in, make *Him* your focus, and see what love will do.

Precious Jesus,

Help me to rid my life of any needless thing that hinders my progress in You. Nothing is worth that. Fan the flame of love in my heart so I can better comprehend Your love for me and for those around me. I long to live a focused, abiding life. At the end of time here on earth, I want it said, "This was a woman who loved Jesus first and foremost." O Lord, kindle that kind of love in my heart. Help me to gain victory over every selfish sin, every bad habit, and every lying thought. I long to live a blameless life before You, and I know this is a noble pursuit. Protect me from arrows of discouragement and doubt. Help me to use my shield of faith to shut down the devil's every attempt to lure me from my place of peace. I am Yours. I will set up camp right next to You. Oh, how I love You! Amen.

Steps Toward Health

- I will wake up every day and ask God to give me a heart set on following Him.

- I will allow Him to conquer every part of my life, even the areas I would rather keep to myself.

- I will take Him at His word and trust Him when my feelings tell me otherwise.

- I will pray and ask God to show me what repeated distractions are in my life.

- I will ask for His strength and wisdom to take care of these things.

- I understand that living a focused, abiding life will not always be easy, and so I will ask God for endurance to run my life's race and to finish strong.

* I will remember that God honors inner beauty. I will resist the temptation to emphasize my outward appearance at the expense of my inner life.

* I will look to the Lord expectantly—counting on Him to take my offerings and do something great with them. I will apply faith to every time I speak, serve, pray, and love. I will do my part with faith, and then look up to Jesus and watch Him work.

TRY THIS

* This week, eliminate media from your "diet." As much as possible, stay away from the TV and computer screen. Use the time to do something more meaningful.

* Make it a regular practice to fast. Buy a book on fasting and do it safely and wisely. Fasting will bring more clarity and focus to your life than you can imagine. (I will suggest these two, though I am sure there are many more: *Fasting for Spiritual Breakthrough* by Elmer L. Towns and *Hunger for God* by John Piper.)

* Regularly take more time to rest in God's presence. Ten minutes of *focused rest* will do far more to rejuvenate you than two hours of TV!

* Read biographies on some of the spiritual greats who went before us, such as Watchman Nee, A.W. Tozer, Charles Finney, Andrew Murray, Hannah Whitall Smith, Thomas à Kempis, and E.M. Bounds.

* Spend more time meditating and praying over small portions of Scripture. Allow the Word to do its work in your heart.

* Bring your thoughts back to God as soon as you realize they've wandered. Make it your pursuit to live in His presence as you walk here on earth (Psalm 116:9).

As we wrap up the section on our spiritual health, let's look at how a life out of balance affects our spiritual health.

Effects of Spiritual Imbalance

✓ *Too much output, not enough input (over-servers):* tired; tend to struggle with self-righteousness, no margin, and little grace; can be judgmental and often lose perspective; relationships often strained

✓ *Too much input, not enough output (over-resters):* unmotivated; lack vision and passion, and can tend to be critical of how the 'servers' are doing things; struggle with feeling disconnected

Balance Application

By now we should have eliminated many of the things that slow us down and have applied the things we've known for so long but have failed to do. By now we should be walking through life more intently, more passionately, and more focused on the Lord and His calling on our lives. We now know what keeps us strong; it is nourishment, response, and rest. When we manage our physical and spiritual life at this level, we will more easily maintain balance. We may have a busy week, but never again a busy "year." We may gain a few pounds, but never again three dress sizes. We may miss a quiet time or two, but never again a whole week. We will manage what God has given us with a much closer eye. We will keep the main things the main things. We will guard our intimacy with God. We will take good care of our loved ones. We will serve as God leads. We will get sufficient exercise. We will protect our times of rest. We will pursue a heart of peace. Life is work. We might as well work at keeping our feet on the ground and our gaze fixed on heaven. As it says in 1 Timothy 4:8, godliness holds promise both in this life and the life to come.

Study Time

1. Read 2 Peter 1:2-4. Verse 2 is my prayer for you. Verse 3 and the first part of verse 4 speak of what we've been provided. What *has* He given us? The latter part of verse 4 tells us two reasons why He has provided these things. Write them down.

2. Can we take hold of one without letting go of the other? Explain.

3. Read 2 Peter 1:5-7. Draw a vertical line. At the bottom, cross the vertical line with a short horizontal line. On that line write "faith." Just above faith, write the virtue this verse tells you to add to your faith. On top of that virtue, write the next one. There should be eight in all. Now look at your vertical line as a wall and look at the stacked virtues as bricks. When you build your life up with these things, you fortify your life. Come back to this question when you have more time and really pray over

these "bricks." Ask God to increase your capacity for every one of them.

4. Read 2 Peter 1:8. Notice the "movement" referred to in this verse. We are called to grow. Based on this verse, what are the positive effects of possessing these qualities?

5. We send our kids to college so that they will be equipped to make a living. We hold our kids accountable so that they will grow in character. We laugh a lot with our kids so that they will not take themselves too seriously. We love our kids immensely so that they will more easily comprehend the love of Christ. This passage from 2 Peter tells us that God has given us everything we need to live a life of power and godliness so that we can participate in His divine nature and thus escape the corruption in the world. We are set up to thrive. The only remaining factor is our yes. Will you say yes to Him today? Will you trust Him with the things that stress you out? Will you believe Him when He says He loves you? Will you follow wherever He leads? Please say yes.

And that about wraps it up. God is strong, and he wants you strong. So take everything the Master has set out for you, well-made weapons of the best materials. And put them to use so you will be able to stand up to everything the Devil throws your way. This is no afternoon athletic contest that we'll walk away from and forget about in a couple of hours. This is for keeps, a life-or-death fight to the finish against the Devil and all his angels. Be prepared. You're up against far more than you can handle on your own. Take all the help you can get, every weapon God has issued, so that when it's all over but the shouting you'll still be on your feet. Truth, righteousness, peace, faith, and salvation are more than words. Learn how to apply them. You'll need them throughout your life. God's Word is an indispensable weapon. In the same way, prayer is essential in this ongoing warfare. Pray hard and long. Pray for your brothers and sisters. Keep your eyes open. Keep each other's spirits up so that no one falls behind or drops out (Ephesians 6:10-18 MSG).

May the Lord make us fit for heaven to live with Him there. Press on, in His name!

Notes

Chapter 5—Be Nourished

1. C.S. Lewis, *Readings for Meditation and Reflection* (New York, NY: Harper Collins, 1992), p. 35.

2. Fasting brings impurities to the surface. If you do end up fasting for more than a day, you will notice a coating on your tongue and potentially an increase in body odor. Because your body isn't being asked to process all of the foods you would normally be eating, it can give itself to the task of purifying your system. We all have toxins in our bodies, and fasting gives our bodies the chance to get rid of them. Some of those toxins will surface on the tongue. Brush regularly and rinse out your mouth. These effects will go away once you start eating again.

Chapter 9—God Enjoys You

1. Brian Simmons, *Song of Songs: The Journey of the Bride* (Tulsa, OK: Insight Publishing Group, 2002), p. 61.

Chapter 11—A Healthy Spiritual Diet

1. If you want an excellent book on fortifying your walls, read Beth Moore's book *When Godly People Do Ungodly Things* (Broadman and Holman Publishers).

2. A.W. Tozer, *The Pursuit of God* (Camp Hill, PA: Christian Publications, 1995), p. 151.

Chapter 12—A Healthy Thought Life

1. Catherine Marshall, *Something More* (Grand Rapids, MI: Chosen Books, 1974), p. 148.

Chapter 13—Spiritual Strength and Endurance

1. Oswald Chambers, *My Utmost for His Highest* (Grand Rapids, MI: Discovery House, 1992), November 18.

Chapter 14—Spiritual "Cardio"

1. Mary Wilder Tileston, *Joy & Strength* (New York: Barnes & Noble, 1993), p. 358.

2. Marshall, *Something More,* p. 153.

3. Frances J. Roberts, *Come Away My Beloved* (Ojai, CA: King's Farspan, Inc., 1970), p. 56.

4. Rick Joyner, *There Were Two Trees in the Garden* (New Kensington, PA: Whitaker House/Morning Star Publications, 1993), pp. 143-44.

5. Chambers, *My Utmost for His Highest,* May 25.

Chapter 15—What Words Do

1. Tozer, *The Pursuit of God: A 31 Day Experience,* pp. 175-76.

Acknowledgments

Special and heartfelt thanks go to:

Chip MacGregor (literary agent extraordinaire), for your encouragement, your friendship, and your expertise; God has used you greatly in my life. I pray that you and Patti will be very blessed in your new endeavors. Thank you for introducing me to Beth Jusino. I know she will be a great agent for me.

My booking agent, Lisa Barry. I am thankful the Lord brought us together!

My friends at Harvest House Publishers. A special thanks to LaRae Weikert. Bless you for believing in this project. And to my editor, Kim Moore. You made the editing process a real joy. Bless you for your servant's heart and your kingdom mind-set.

The wonderful ministry of Hearts at Home. Thank you for granting me the privilege of serving with you. Keep up your high standard. You are making a difference!

My editor friends at Focus on the Family—Jesse, Susan, and Andrea. Thank you for allowing me to work with you.

Yvonne Lehman and the Blue Ridge Mountain Writers Conference, where I learned much about writing and met a few lifelong friends (Vonda, Peggy, and Helen).

Terri Blackstock, Peggy Stoks, Luke Hinrichs, and Christopher Soderstrom, who helped me get started in writing. I will always be grateful that you made time for me. May God richly bless you for your kindness.

Francis Frangipane. You have shaped my thinking more than any other contemporary author. I quote you every time I speak.

My team of intercessors, who cover me in prayer prior, during, and after all of my speaking engagements. May you be allowed to see the fruit of your prayers.

My readers (and dear friends) who spent hours reviewing my rough drafts—Peggy and Mark Kohler (Mark, thanks for the "10 Steps" idea.), Patty Fischer, Bonnie Newberg, Judy Chesla, Daryl and Digger Jackson, Cindy Larson, Peggy Stoks, Susan Stuart, Dave Plaep, Linda Larson, Kay

Blake, and Andie Munn. Thank you, Cherrill Warren, for putting hours into reading *and* research so I could make my deadline. Bless you all for your time and your helpful insights.

Sandi Elsmore, for your volunteer work.

Lu Herbeck of the National Exercise Trainers Association. Thank you for your input and your friendship. You were a wonderful boss.

Dr. Jim Abeler and Jan Peters, for your input on the power of rest. Bless you for your time.

My parents, Ed and Pat Erickson, for your never-ending love and support. I love you to pieces.

My three precious teenage sons—Jake, Luke, and Jordan. You fill my life with such joy and sunshine. I thank my Lord every time I think of you.

My unbelievable husband, Kevin. This year we will celebrate our twentieth anniversary, and I adore you more now than the day I first said yes to you. Bless you, honey, for your strong presence in my life. I love you more than words can say.

Jesus, my One and Only. You have redeemed and restored every area of my life. I love You most.

How to Contact the Author

Susie Larson is a popular speaker, a freelance writer for Focus on the Family, and an author. She has been certified with the American Council on Exercise since 1991. She and her husband, Kevin, have three teenage boys and make their home in Minnesota.

Susie may be contacted at:

c/o Harvest House Publishers
990 Owen Loop North
Eugene, OR 97402

Or by e-mail at: info@susielarson.com

Other Good
Harvest House Reading

A WOMAN'S SECRET TO A BALANCED LIFE
Lysa TerKeurst and *Sharon Jaynes*

From the leadership of Proverbs 31 Ministries comes this essential book, offering seven vital ways any Christian woman can prioritize her life more effectively.

THE 10 BEST DECISIONS A WOMAN CAN MAKE
Pam Farrel

Bestselling author Pam Farrel encourages women to exchange the fleeting standards of the world for the steadfast truths found in a growing, fruitful relationship with God as they find their place in His plan.

ORDINARY MOM, EXTRAORDINARY GOD
Mary DeMuth

Stay-at-home mom Mary DeMuth offers a devotional aimed at the deeper issues of the heart and one that will provide a soothing respite amid chaos. Think of it as Oswald Chambers meets Busy Housewife.

WHEN WOMEN LONG FOR REST
Cindi McMenamin

Women today want to break away from the demands of life and rest at God's feet to experience true rest. Here, they'll discover the secrets to avoiding spiritual burnout and enjoying greater intimacy with God.

BEING A WISE WOMAN IN A WILD WORLD
Robin Chaddock

What is wisdom? It's living minute by minute in God's eternal love. Robin helps women use their unique gifts to understand the principles of wise living and draw closer to God by pursuing His wisdom.

HARVEST HOUSE
PUBLISHERS

The Hearts at Home organization is committed to meeting the needs of women in the profession of motherhood. Founded in 1993, Hearts at Home offers a variety of resources and events to assist women in their jobs as wives and mothers.

Find out how Hearts at Home can provide you with ongoing education and encouragement in the profession of motherhood. In addition to this book, our resources include the *Hearts at Home* magazine, the *Hearts at Home* devotional, and our Hearts at Home website. Additionally, Hearts at Home events make a great getaway for individuals, moms groups, or for that special friend, sister, or sister-in-law. The regional conferences, attended by over ten thousand women each year, provide a unique, affordable, and highly encouraging weekend for the woman who takes the profession of motherhood seriously.

Hearts at Home
900 W. College Ave.
Normal, Illinois 61761
Fax: (309) 888-4525
Email: hearts@hearts-at-home.org